WHAT ARE *YOUR* REASONS FOR NOT ENJOYING LIFE RIGHT NOW?

- I'll have fun after I make enough money
- I haven't found the right person to love
- I'm too fat/tall/short/unattractive/shy/nervous
- My parents ruined my life
- My husband/wife upsets me
- My boss isn't fair
- The world is in terrible shape
- The government is run by corrupt politicians

WOULD YOU LIKE TO HAVE MORE PLEASURE, MORE FRIENDS, MORE GOOD TIMES, MORE SATISFACTION, AND MORE FULFILLMENT STARTING IMMEDIATELY AND CONTINUING EACH AND EVERY DAY FOR THE REST OF YOUR LIFE?

YOU CAN. FIND OUT HOW.

LIFE IS UNCERTAIN . . . EAT DESSERT FIRST!

"A rare and highly original se''help book that uniquely stresses happiness as well as s .ty. Sensible and joyous reading! " — Albert Ellis, Ph.D., President, Institute for Rational-Emotive Therapy, New York City

QUANTITY SALES

Most Dell books are available at special quantity discounts when purchased in bulk by corporations, organizations, or groups. Special imprints, messages, and excerpts can be produced to meet your needs. For more information, write to: Dell Publishing, 1540 Broadway, New York, NY 10036. Attention: Special Markets.

INDIVIDUAL SALES

Are there any Dell books you want but cannot find in your local stores? If so, you can order them directly from us. You can get any Dell book currently in print. For a complete up-to-date listing of our books and information on how to order, write to: Dell Readers Service, Box DR, 1540 Broadway, New York, NY 10036.

LIFE IS UNCERTAIN ... EAT DESSERT FIRST!

Finding the Joy You Deserve

Sol Gordon and Harold Brecher

A DELL BOOK

Published by
Dell Publishing
a division of
Bantam Doubleday Dell Publishing Group, Inc.
1540 Broadway
New York, New York 10036

Life Is Uncertain . . . Eat Dessert First! used by permission of Sizzler Restaurants.
"Oh, How I Hate to Get Up and Get Going" and "Whine, Whine, Whine!" by Dr.
Albert Ellis reprinted by permission of the author and Institute for Rational-Emotive
Therapy.
DIRECT DECISION THERAPY © 1973 Dr. Harold Greenwald. Reprinted by permis-
ion of the author.
ENJOY YOURSELF (IT'S LATER THAN YOU THINK) by Herb Magidson and Carl
Sigman: © 1948, 1949 EDWIN H. MORRIS & COMPANY, A Division of MPL Commu-
nications, Inc. © Renewed 1976, 1977 EDWIN H. MORRIS & COMPANY, A division
of MPL Communications, Inc. International Copyright Secured. All Rights Reserved.
HAPPY TALK by Richard Rodgers and Oscar Hammerstein II: © 1949 by Richard
Rodgers and Oscar Hammerstein II. Copyright renewed WILLIAMSON MUSIC CO.,
Owner of Publication and Allied Rights. Used by permission. All Rights Reserved.
HEADING HOME by Paul Tsongas: © 1984 by Paul Tsongas. Reprinted by permis-
sion of Alfred A. Knopf, Inc.
HEALTHY PLEASURES by Dr. Robert Ornstein and Dr. David Sobel: © 1989. Re-
printed by permission of Addison-Wesley Publishing Co, Inc.
DEAR ABBY by Abigail Van Buren: © Abigail Van Buren, United Press Syndicate.

The trademark Dell® is registered in the U.S. Patent and Trademark
Office.

ISBN: 0-440-20867-X

Reprinted by arrangement with Delacorte Press

Printed in the United States of America

Published simultaneously in Canada

April 1996

10 9 8 7 6 5 4 3 2 1
OPM

LIFE IS UNCERTAIN ... EAT DESSERT FIRST!

Contents

A PERSON
WILL BE CALLED TO ACCOUNT
ON JUDGMENT DAY
FOR EVERY PERMISSIBLE THING
HE MIGHT HAVE ENJOYED
BUT DID NOT
    —THE TALMUD

Introduction

Recently, stores have been jam-packed with a glut of message-bearing novelties—buttons, aprons, T-shirts, refrigerator magnets, posters, greeting cards, bumper stickers—all sporting some version of the dictum to take pleasure when and where you can: "Don't worry—BE HAPPY!" ... "ENJOY LIFE NOW!—This Is Not a Dress Rehearsal" ... "LIVING WELL IS THE BEST REVENGE" ... "GO FIRST CLASS or Your Heirs Will" ... "We're Driving Around Enjoying Our Children's Inheritance" ... "Life's Uncertain—EAT DESSERT FIRST!"

Why this sudden focus on enjoyment?

The fact is, the universal desire for living joyfully is nothing new. Poets and philosophers have long wrestled with the subject. What is new is the urgency of the desire and the feverish fervor with which people approach pleasure.

Social psychologists report that TV is largely responsible for the increased craving for pleasure. They may be right. Can anyone honestly say, after viewing thousands of scenes of people really living it up, they haven't at times questioned the lackluster quality of their lives?

Where do we get the notion that life should be one big blast? Check out TV: Win or lose, game-show contestants and audiences shriek with joy. Fans explode with glee at sporting events. From Donahue to Geraldo, talk shows feature experts who preach the gospel of heaven on earth—and deliver the definitive word on attaining more joyful satisfaction in relationships, careers, marriage, parenthood, sex.

Commercials are particularly joy-oriented. Ads routinely depict people getting their kicks from such humdrum activities as shampooing their hair, brushing their teeth, eating a breakfast cereal, or washing their clothes, windows, or floors. Advertisers have no shame—they portray such bothersome tasks as gassing up the family car and calling in an exterminator as near-bliss experiences; their spokesmen get carried away with the ecstasy of discovering a butter substitute, a microwavable gourmet dinner, and a mold-vanquishing bathroom cleanser.

One beer commercial equates guzzling suds with sublime joy as groups of exuberant sportsmen, reveling in camaraderie, drink up to the theme: "It doesn't get any better than this."

TV has indeed intensified age-old concerns and has heightened timeworn expectations, and as a consequence millions believe they're misfits because they don't enjoy life more fully.

There's a good side and a bad side to TV's pleasure-bent bias. The good side: heightened expectations stimulate desire and motivation. The bad side: disappointment and depression ensue when quick-fix fun activities fail to live up to expectations.

To enjoy life more fully we must increase our ability to

gladden our *moment-by-moment* and *day-to-day* experiences—and that's what this book is all about.

Since a heavy heart is the most serious form of overweightedness, *Eat Dessert First!* may be the ultimate diet book.

SOL GORDON AND HAROLD BRECHER

You work and work for years and years.
You're always on the go.
You never take a minute off,
too busy making dough.

Some day you say you'll have your fun
when you're a millionaire.
Imagine all the fun you'll have
in your old rockin' chair.

ENJOY YOURSELF,
it's later than you think;
ENJOY YOURSELF,
while you're still in the pink.

The years go by
as quickly as a wink.
ENJOY YOURSELF, ENJOY YOURSELF,
it's later than you think.

"Enjoy Yourself"
Words by Herb Magidson
Music by Carl Sigman
Copyright by Magidson Music Co., Inc.

RULE ONE

When Living Hurts, Joy Relieves the Pain

We hold these truths to be self-evident,
that all men are created equal,
that they are endowed by their Creator
with certain unalienable Rights,
that among these are Life, Liberty,
and the PURSUIT OF HAPPINESS.

from the Declaration of Independence
in Congress, July 4, 1776

1

Enjoy! Enjoy!

Life is difficult—filled with problems and pain—and when living hurts, joy eases the strain.

As he approached the Gates of Heaven, Elmo Rantin believed he had it made.

"This is going to be a piece of cake," he told himself. "I've paid my dues. I've been a good son, husband, and father, put my family first, remembered to have my secretary send birthday and anniversary presents to my wife, and never stayed late at the office without giving her a call. I've earned a good living, only took legitimate deductions on my tax returns, left my family well fixed, and have given to charity."

"But did you enjoy yourself?" asked the admitting angel.

"Not as much as some people, but who had the time?" asked Elmo.

"Sorry, we don't admit your kind," said the angel.

"You're kidding," Elmo argued, astonished. "I was a better-than-average guy. I gave up pleasures for the sake of my family. I worked hard and sacrificed. I always let my wife drive the new car. I've forgiven everyone who did me dirt—almost. Not admit me? Why?"

"Because," the angel explained, "there's no room in heaven for people who haven't fully enjoyed themselves on earth. I'm sorry, but you'll have to go back and do it all over again."

One of Sol's students, after hearing this parable, said, "Dr. Gordon, aside from showing how unjust people in power can be and that even angels can be terribly unfair, I think the story is pointless. I'm sure Elmo would have preferred to enjoy life more, but why ban him from heaven when he probably couldn't help himself?"

"Careful," Sol said. "Can you be certain Elmo never wasted time in unrewarding activities? That he didn't put pleasure aside because of ambition, guilt-ridden anxieties, or misplaced priorities?"

"Weeeell," the student said.

End of conversation.

While we can't be positive we've been put on earth to carry out the Talmudic advice to achieve joyfulness, there's no doubt we'd lead happier lives if we assumed this were so.

Though closely related, happiness and joy are not the same. Happiness is the term used to describe a long-term state of contentment, well-being, and good feeling. Joy, on the other hand, is more elusive, temporary, fleeting—now you have it, now you don't. When joy outweighs sadness, people consider themselves happy.

However, while joy, like money, facilitates happiness—it's actually harder to come by than money!

Attaining more joy, then, is the first step toward happiness, and that's what *Eat Dessert First!* is all about—increasing your ability to enjoy yourself.

And to do it *before* Judgment Day.

Sad to say, if you are not *fully* enjoying life, for whatever reason, you've got lots of company!

Lois M., a twenty-nine-year-old department-store jewelry buyer, prefers to stay home alone than go anywhere without a date. "All my friends are on their second marriages, and I haven't had my first," she whines. "I guess when it comes to romance, I'm just cursed."

Becky L., a wealthy widow, lives in a high-rise condo, with a magnificent view of the Florida Gulf Coast. When friends ask her to join them on cruises, Elderhostel vacations, and sightseeing tours, she hesitates over the cost, then refuses, saying, "Who needs it? I'll see those fancy-schmancy places on TV."

Ike O., a supermarket assistant produce manager, moonlights as a security guard and has taken a third job on weekends, tending bar at a disco. "Financial security first, fun later," he tells his wife when she complains they never get to go anywhere or do anything anymore.

Robert Q. is a thirty-seven-year-old "couch potato," ever ready with a reason not to leave the house. Parties? "A frivolous waste of time." Dining out? "The service is terrible these days—and so is the food." A movie? "All the new films are made for five-year-old mental retards."

Shirley S., a divorcée who now lives with her parents, has let her looks go since she and her husband broke up. When her family prompts her to get out in the social swim and start having some fun again, she promises, "I will—just as soon as I lose some weight and can buy myself some nice new clothes."

Trish P., a top producer with a high-powered real estate firm, is a superachiever and so extremely competitive that she rarely does anything "just for fun." Recently, a friend talked her into taking an afternoon off—to shop, have lunch, take in a movie—and as they parted, asked, "Did you have a good time?" "Not really," said Trish. "We really didn't accomplish anything, did we?"

Why do so many people, blessed with seemingly fortunate circumstances, miss out on joyousness while others, struggling under extremely trying conditions, embrace life with exuberance?

Two cases in point—the people we've dedicated this book to:

Phyllis Hoffman is a single parent who struggled and sacrificed to put two kids through college. No sooner had they graduated when tragedy struck. First breast cancer and a mastectomy; then, just as she thought she'd passed the five-year "cured" period, the discovery that the cancer had spread to her lungs, bones, and liver. Doctors gave up; Phyllis didn't. She investigated experimental treatments, and for the past six years has subjected herself to harsh therapies that have kept her weak, nauseous, subject to high fever and infections—but alive.

None of it has dampened her spirits. An editorial assistant, she faces each workday with enthusiasm. Three or four evenings a week she enjoys the company of friends—either visiting, dining out, or taking in a concert or movie. She makes plans—for get-togethers with her kids, a trip to Europe, a holiday visit with her brother's family in Florida. When asked to account for her high-spirited life-style, she admits, "Believe me, sometimes I do get depressed, but it doesn't last long. Life is too short to waste on self-pity. It sounds corny, but I get a kick out of simple things like getting home from work, taking off my shoes, working the crossword puzzle, or taking a walk through the park. I enjoy every moment I'm alive."

Following his near-fatal automobile accident, sixty-eight-year-old Irving Tenenbaum was in a coma, and doctors had all but given him up for dead. "Maybe it's time to pull the plug," they suggested as years went by without any visible improvement in his condition.

His wife, Joan, however, refused to give up hope. All through the ordeal she behaved as though Irving were conscious of everything going on around him. She talked to him, played his favorite music, tuned in his favorite TV shows.

Even more remarkable, she maintained her sense of humor and never missed celebrating a holiday or Irving's birthdays. Guests picked up on her lightheartedness and joked along with her.

Three and a half years dragged by—and then one day Irving woke up. He was able to speak, made good sense, and had partial use of his hands.

When asked how she managed to handle the "dark days"

with such optimism, Joan says, "I prayed a lot and just knew things would work out for the best.

"I suppose some people thought I was some kind of kook—laughing and pretending nothing was wrong. But that's their problem. I truly believe it's what kept Irving alive and me from losing my mind."

Life is an obstacle course. There isn't a person we know who hasn't wrestled with legitimate concerns or does not have problems that subject him to periodic worry, anxiety, and grief. There are lots of reasons for people to be unhappy—some of them serious, such as ill health, the loss of loved ones, financial and career setbacks, unexpected disasters; others are trivial, such as losing your keys, missing a party, finding out a friend is gossiping about you, having it rain on your parade.

But why are some able to roll with life's punches while others are crushed by relatively minor setbacks?

Know one thing: problems are part of the human condition—life *is* uncertain.

While you cannot pick and choose which mixture of thorny experiences will come along to challenge you, you can choose the spirit with which you handle them.

The essential questions remain:

WHY are some lighthearted while others take life so seriously?

WHY do some find it easy to enjoy life while others have so hard a time experiencing pleasure?

WHY are some folks joy-oriented while others are joy-resistant?

One reason that has long been overlooked is our individual capacity for joyfulness. Just as some people are genetically predisposed toward obesity, many have inherited the burden of a heavy heart.

To determine *your* potential for joy, take this quiz, then check the analysis that follows.

JOY CAPACITY QUIZ

Question 1. In each of the following three groupings choose the statement that comes closest to how your parents might describe what you were like as a child.

GROUP #1

(A) "... a good child; attentive; hardly gave me any trouble."

(B) "... a terror; had a mind of his own; was always up to some mischief."

(C) "... a confusing child; an angel one day, a devil the next."

GROUP #2

(A) "... a busy little mind; curious and adventuresome."

(B) "... a love; never wandered off, was always at my side."

(C) "... a serious child; anxious and cautious."

GROUP #3

(A) "... didn't make friends easily."

(B) "... was always getting into fights."

(C) "... had lots of friends."

Question #2. You believe you'd be a more joyful or successful person today if your parents had been more loving, patient, and supportive.
(A) Yes (B) No (C) Maybe

Question #3. In each of the following three groupings, choose the statement that best describes you now.

GROUP #1

    (A) "Superinvolved—I wish there were more hours in a day."

    (B) "I'm bored—nothing seems to excite me anymore."

    (C) "Frustrated—people keep sabotaging my efforts."

GROUP #2

    (A) "I'm a bit apprehensive about an upcoming change."

        (Example: a move to a new community, new job, getting married, divorced, pregnant, buying a house.)

    (B) "I'm so fearful about an upcoming change that I can't sleep at night."

    (C) "I'm so anxious about an upcoming change that I lose my cool."

GROUP #3

    (A) "I've never really needed friends all that much."

    (B) "Life would be *impossible* without friends."

    (C) "Friends make life more interesting and joyful."

Question #4. I (A) frequently (B) rarely (C) always solicit advice before making an important decision.

Question #5. I am (or was) on (A) good (B) fair (C) poor terms with my parents.

Question #6. When I meet people, it takes me (A) no time at all (B) a while (C) a long time to warm up to them.

Question #7. When I think about the progress I've made in improving my lot in life, I (A) often (B) sometimes (C) rarely feel as though I'm spinning my wheels.

Question #8. I'm usually (A) delighted (B) suspicious (C) embarrassed when I receive an unexpected compliment.

Question #9. I (A) frequently (B) often (C) rarely regret having said (or not said) something.

SCORING

Question #1

GROUP #1:
(B) 2 points; (C) 1 point; (A) ½ point
GROUP #2:
(A) 2 points; (B) 1 point; (C) ½ point
GROUP #3:
(C) 2 points; (B) 1 point; (A) ½ point

Question #2
(C) 4 points; (B) 2 points; (A) 1 point

Question #3
GROUP #1:
(A) 4 points; (C) 2 points; (B) 1 point
GROUP #2:
(A) 4 points; (C) 2 points; (B) 1 point
GROUP #3:
(C) 4 points; (A) 2 points; (B) 1 point

Question #4:
   (B) 2 points; (A) 1 point; (C) ½ point

Question #5:
   (A) 4 points; (B) 2 points; (C) 1 point

Question #6:
   (A) 4 points; (B) 2 points; (C) 1 point

Question #7:
   (C) 4 points; (B) 2 points; (A) 1 point

Question #8:
   (A) 4 points; (C) 2 points; (B) 1 point

Question #9:
   (C) 4 points; (B) 2 points; (A) 1 point

ANALYSIS

If you scored—

37 to 44 points: You have an EXCELLENT potential for joy and will find it easy to enjoy life even more as time goes by.

28 to 36 points: You have a GOOD potential for joy and will have to exert only moderate effort to enjoy life more.

19 to 27 points: You have a FAIR potential for joy and will have to make some changes and work at it to get more pleasure from life.

11 to 18 points: You need to read this book carefully and make an all-out effort to turn your life around!

Okay, now that you know your joy potential, where does that get you? What is this thing called Joy?

JOY IS . . .

. . . a momentary state of being, ranging from pleasure to euphoria, which accompanies blissful experiences that are not harmful or hurtful to oneself or to others (not to be included: taking drugs, overeating, abusing yourself or anyone else).

You can experience joy with such diverse activities as watching the sunset over the volcanic cliffs of Kauai, teaching your six-year-old to ride his two-wheeler without training wheels, or reading the latest gossip in the *National Enquirer*.

JOY nourishes self-esteem, and joyful persons are more likely to like themselves, feel accountable for their behavior, and respect the rights and feelings of others.

JOYFUL PEOPLE . . .

- . . . experience joy frequently. (Only seriously disturbed individuals enjoy everything all the time.)
- . . . are comfortable with people.
- . . . adjust to change easily.
- . . . are undaunted by challenges and open to new ideas.
- . . . rarely blame or complain.
- . . . enjoy a wide variety of pleasurable activities.
- . . . savor such things as seasonal changes, the smell of newly cut grass, a healthy bowel movement.

... take pride in and celebrate major and minor accomplishments—their own and the achievements of others.

... recall the good times but don't dwell on the past.

... are in control of their lives yet don't feel compelled to control others'.

... are a joy to be with.

... maintain long-term friendships.

... accept responsibility for their happiness.

... may experience inner joy without showing it, or

... may express joy exuberantly.

... are occasionally subject to loneliness, anger, and depression, but

... are able to shake off such conditions quickly. How quickly? Too long a time is no good. Less is all right.

... manage to live within their means and are not plagued by financial concerns as are people who overspend.

... are straightforward and rarely pretend to be something they're not.

... can give of themselves without expecting anything in return.

... are serious when appropriate.

... are deeply concerned with the welfare of others, yet are still able to enjoy life.

RULE TWO

To Be More Joyful
You Must Accept
Responsibility for
Your Happiness

WHINE, WHINE, WHINE!*
(to be sung to the tune of "The Wiffenpoof Song")

I cannot have all my wishes filled—
Whine, whine, whine!
I cannot have every frustration stilled—
Whine, whine, whine!
Life really owes me the things I miss,
Fate has to grant me eternal bliss!
And if I must settle for less than this—
Whine, whine, whine!

> Lyrics by Dr. Albert Ellis,
> founder of the Institute for Rational-Emotive
> Therapy.

*From "A Garland of Rational Songs," published by the Institute for Rational-Emotive Therapy.

2

The Roots of Joylessness
Nature vs. Nurture vs. God Knows What

In all Sol's years as a psychologist he's yet to counsel an individual who wasn't firmly convinced that an external cause—a deprived childhood, inauspicious education, inadequate parenting, ill-starred event, alien influences, or just pure bad luck—is responsible for his or her unhappiness.

Most people we know are locked into the conviction that something outside themselves prevents them from achieving optimal joy.

Their minds are set. They hold their upbringing, genes, or fate responsible for their unhappy predicaments. And once so convinced, they are stuck.

MIND-SET AND JOYLESSNESS

It's not until mind-sets are shocked loose—until joyless persons abandon finding someone or something to *blame*—that

15

they're able to accept greater responsibility for their unhappiness and take the steps necessary to enjoy life more fully.

In research on divorce it was found that men and women who blame their marital failure on their ex-spouses suffer longer than those who see many possible explanations for their breakup.

In research on loneliness it was found that lonelies who believe their aloneness is fated—there were perhaps bad planetary aspects the day they were born—stay lonely longer. Moreover, people who believe they are the victim of circumstances, much like pawns on a giant chessboard being moved around by unseen hands, stay unhappy longer when things don't go their way.

On the other side, alcoholics who are convinced the cause of their problem is solely genetic seem to give up the control that could help them recover. The overweight who are positive they are genetically predisposed toward obesity are the ones most likely to ditch their diets. People who say "I was born this way" are unlikely to expend the effort to rid themselves of destructive habits.

In the midst of a group therapy discussion updating the nature-versus-nurture controversy, during which Sol presented the genetic side of the argument, Marilyn L., usually a mild-mannered and well-behaved participant, became surprisingly vitriolic.

"I think all this is a lot of crap," she shrieked, "invented by some egghead shrinks who had nothing better to do with their time."

"Why all the anger?" Sol asked.

"It makes absolutely no sense," she said. "We don't come into this world with developed personalities."

Sol told her she'd misunderstood him; people aren't born with full-blown personalities, but many studies of infants have indeed revealed they have differing personality characteristics at birth.

She wasn't buying any of it. "When you hit me with the statement that some babies are born happier than others, you really got to me."

Since he'd obviously struck a raw nerve, Sol asked her to explain why she was so incensed.

"Because when kids are unhappy, it's because of their parents—not their genes!"

Sol told her it wasn't an either/or proposition—that parents can indeed make children unhappy and that infants can be born with a sorrowful bent that makes it more likely they'll develop into unhappy adults.

She thought for a while and grumbled, "I'll think about it."

About a week later Marilyn came to see him and said, "You know, Dr. Gordon, that genetic stuff is beginning to make sense."

"Oh?" he said.

"I've always blamed my parents for my unhappiness," she confessed. "They divorced when I was only seven, and for the next five years or so I was shuttled back and forth between them, always wishing and hoping we'd be a real family again someday.

"Then, when first my mom, and then my dad, remarried, things got really hairy. I had stepparents, half-brothers, and half-sisters, and felt I had no real place in the world and no one really cared about me.

"Ever since then I've blamed them for everything that went wrong in my life, but I talked to my grandma the other day and told her what you said. According to her I was born with a 'weltschmerz'—a sadness with the world—and was an unhappy baby right from the start.

"She said I was a grim toddler, moody during my high-chair days, and it took a lot to make me laugh even when I was just an infant. So maybe it's not entirely my parents' fault that I feel the way I do—maybe my parents did the best they could, and it's up to me to find a way to be happy despite it all."

Marilyn had learned something that will stand her in good stead for the rest of her life—*to achieve joy, you must first challenge your mind-set.*

Once she gave up automatically excusing her unhappiness in such a single-minded way, she was able to let go of the justifications that supported her mind-set.

SHAKING YOUR MIND-SET FREE

It's ironic, but true—the less certain you are of the root of your unhappiness, the better your chance of moving toward greater joyfulness.

So let's hit you where it hurts.

Of all the many reasons people of all ages fall back on to justify being unhappy, parents lead the hit list. "It's the way I was brought up" is such a fixed belief, it's an almost automatic response.

Despite the persuasive evidence that genetics is a significant personality determinant, millions doggedly insist on pinpointing environmental factors as primarily responsible for their personality failings and subsequent unhappiness.

Why? It's easier to scapegoat your upbringing than to accept responsibility for your happiness (or unhappiness). Without "mean" mothers, "distant" fathers, "deprived" childhoods to take to task and rebuke for joylessness, many would have to take a long look in the mirror—and that might be too painful.

Also, the environmental explanation makes for better conversation. "My mother programmed me for failure" is apt to get you more attention and sympathy than "I've been a lazy son of a gun since the day I was born."

MOM AND DAD WERE RIGHT

Scientists are now discovering what many moms and dads have known from observation—that some infants come into this world more joyful than others, and the joy-related personality traits they're born with are apt to stay with them their entire lives.

From the outset, and to varying degrees, some babies are fearless, adventuresome, and fun loving, while others arrive as anxious, timid, and serious little people. Though born with the inalienable right to pursue joy, each of us is in fact created with unequal potentials for enjoyment.

Of course there are children who are born "happy" and are crushed by abusive parenting. Among families you know you must have noticed maladjusted children who seem to have really good, caring, and loving parents—and quite well adjusted children who've thrived despite neglect and inadequate parenting.

NATURE VS. NURTURE

Which has the greater impact on personality and behavior? Is it inherited genes or is it environment—parental, peer, and cultural influences?

We really don't know how much influence genetics has on

behavior. Even geneticists acknowledge that traits such as agreeableness or "niceness" appear to be uninfluenced by genetics.

Although there's as yet no definitive answer, a growing body of evidence suggests that we each have a strong genetic predisposition toward particular characteristics—and that includes a potential for enjoyment that may be set before we take our first breath.

What we all inherit is our nervous system—and if it is fragile, there are severe limits to how much stress we can tolerate. Certain individuals are born survivors; they can withstand life's toughest blows and emerge with their sunny dispositions intact. Others crumble in the face of adversity, growing ever more grouchy, grumbling, and gloomy with every minor inconvenience.

We know genes are a factor. But, when you get right down to it, you bear the ultimate responsibility for experiencing or not experiencing joy.

GENETIC UPDATE

The most significant findings on psychological genetics come from the Minnesota Center for Twin and Adoption Research. Since 1979, researchers have tested 348 sets of twins, including 44 pairs of identical twins raised separately—many from birth on. Their findings: Seven important personality traits associated with joyfulness are primarily genetically determined: extroversion, conformity, worry, creativity, paranoia, optimism, cautiousness.

The Ohio "Jim" twins—Jim Springer and Jim Lewis—are perhaps the most publicized case of identical twins separated in infancy. When they met after having been apart for thirty-nine years, their test scores on such personality variables as tolerance, conformity, flexibility, self-control, and sociability were so close, it was as if the same person had taken the test twice.

What's more, it was found that both Jims enjoy woodworking, chain-smoking Salems, stock-car racing, and vacationing at the same Florida Gulf Coast beach.

Genetics have even been found to be an important factor in job satisfaction. Twins raised apart show a matching tendency to be happy or unhappy in the workplace. They not only gravitate toward similar jobs, but also hold similar attitudes toward their work.

The bottom line: Identical twins raised in vastly different environments turn out much the same, supporting the proposition that if you were anxious and joyless at birth, you're apt to be an anxious and less joyful adult, and if you were relaxed and joyful at birth, you've got a head start on living a relaxed and joy-filled life.

Our admitted purpose in presenting and underscoring this data on genetics is to shake you up, to force you to question your conviction as to the importance of environmental factors, to goad you into action. Not until you adopt a more open-minded attitude toward your own behavior and attitude can real change become possible.

Compelling as the research is, however, the implications are not as grim as they might seem. There is nothing in the data that says genetic influences cannot be overcome. They can. If your inborn potential for joy is limited, take heart. With courage, determination, and some help you can turn things around and learn to enjoy life to the fullest.

YOU CAN OUTGROW JOYLESSNESS

Even joyless babies can turn into joy-filled adults.

Ellen S. was an anxious infant—shy and cautious. She would hide from newcomers and cling to her mother whenever strangers appeared.

When she reached adolescence, pubescent body changes shattered her self-image. She stopped growing, her breasts became pendulous, and she began putting on weight. The once cute preteen metamorphosed into an overly mature-looking high-schooler. Her classmates snickered and made rude remarks. To worsen matters her father earned a promotion that called for a move to a new city. Ellen, bitter, self-conscious, and unable to make new friends in a strange school, blamed her parents for her misery—and for a dreary school life, a disappointing career choice, a bad first marriage, and never being able to wear size-eight designer jeans.

Ellen is now remarried, and has two children, each so different from the other that they have challenged her conviction that parents are totally responsible for their children's happiness. Allison is a happy, outgoing five-year-old with a smile that just won't quit; Justine, only a year younger, is gloomy, cautious, and suspicious.

Unable to explain their differences in terms of her influence, Ellen has begun to question her beliefs and is shedding some of her bitterness toward her parents. Like a child learning to walk, Ellen has taken a first step toward accepting responsibility for her happiness.

RULE THREE

The Less You Justify Joylessness The More You'll Enjoy Life

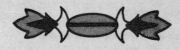

Talk about a moon
floatin' in de sky,
lookin' like a lily on a lake;

Talk about a bird
learnin' how to fly,
makin' all de music he can make.

Happy talk,
keep talkin' happy talk,
Talk about things you'd like to do!

You gotta have a dream
If you don't have a dream,

how you gonna have a dream come true?

If you don't talk happy
n' you never have a dream,
den you'll never have a dream come true!

"Happy Talk"
Music by Richard Rodgers
Words by Oscar Hammerstein II

From the show *South Pacific*
in which a young Polynesian girl
and her mother try to tell an American boy
how to enjoy life.

3

Joystifications

Dr. Elisabeth Kübler-Ross, a noted gerontologist, tells of a terminally ill eighty-five-year-old patient who looked back on her life and said, "God, if I had my life to live over, I would dare more mistakes next time, I would relax and ramble around and would be sillier than I have been this trip. I would take fewer things so seriously and take more chances. I would take more trips and climb more mountains and swim more rivers. I would eat more ice cream and less prunes.

"I would perhaps have more actual troubles, but I sure would have fewer imaginary ones. You see, I am one of those people who lived sensibly and safely, hour after hour, day after day. Oh, I have had my moments, and if I had to do it over again, I would have more of them. In fact, I would try to have nothing else—just moments, one after another—instead of living so many years in a big chair, acting like all of those

persons who never go anywhere without a thermometer, a hot
water bottle, a raincoat, a parachute.

"If I had to do it again, *I would come lighter next time. If I
had to live my life over, I would start backward, early spring
instead of waiting till the fall* [our emphasis].

"I would go to more dances. I would ride more merry-go-
rounds. I would pick more daisies."

... a bittersweet reminder that life is too short and uncertain
for us to miss out on attainable pleasures.

But you need not be facing death to regret a lifetime of
justifications for putting pleasures on hold.

Humans are blessed with wondrous brains capable of devel-
oping miracle vaccines, deducing ways to travel to the heavens
and back ... and concocting rational-sounding excuses for
joylessness.

Ordinarily, justifications defend a decision or behavior. Justifications that validate *joylessness* would more appropriately be
called "JOYstifications."

JUSTIFICATIONS VS. JOYSTIFICATIONS

After suffering a setback, being disappointed by a friend,
losing someone or something precious, or even anticipating
something dreadful, it's normal to become saddened, anxious,
ill-tempered, or depressed. Justificatons help us explain our
response to ourselves and to others.

However, when we persist in justifying such setbacks or
resort to justifications to explain away an ongoing joylessness,
they become self-defeating "joystifications."

Justifications help you defend and clarify your point of view
or course of action and have little effect on your ability to enjoy

yourself. For example: When you justify a purchase ("It was a bargain"), vote for a candidate ("He's got a good record on civil rights"), loan a friend money ("She'd do the same for me if I asked"), change jobs ("You have to move around to move ahead"), you crystallize your thinking and bolster your self-confidence.

Joystifications, on the other hand, are emotionally based cop-outs—pseudoreasonable defenses to explain away negative responses. Chronic joystifying diminishes your ability to enjoy life.

When you joystify feelings of unhappiness ("I got taken by a used car dealer"; "My friend let me down"; "The new boss is a tyrant") you legitimize joylessness and give it a stranglehold on your psyche. Even when valid, repeated joystifications lead to chronic displeasure.

Justifications are primarily intellectual exercises and can be changed with reason. Joystifications are emotionally based and difficult to dislodge.

Put simply, justifications have little or no lasting effect on joy, whereas joystifying keeps you mired in joylessness.

With the giant wooden horse completed, the weather just right, and with goddess Athena's support, General Epeius still couldn't decide which lieutenant was best qualified to lead his warriors to storm Troy's gates.

While asleep the answer came to him. He'd order each of the candidates to submit a list of reasons why Operation Trojan Horse should be delayed.

At dawn he gathered his lieutenants and instructed them to list all the reasons they could think of for putting off the attack.

After the lists were submitted and tallied, Epeius announced, "Since Lieutenant Joyus has the least number of reasons for delaying this venture, he will lead the attack."

At that, Lieutenant Nobrainus stood up and screamed, "Miscount! Miscount! I had nothing on my list. *Nothing*. Zero, zip, zilch. I should lead the group!"

"Fool!" barked Epeius. "Anyone who couldn't come up with even one reason to delay an obviously risky venture doesn't have enough sense to come in out of the rain!"

Nobrainus was demoted to private and relegated to the kitchen, where he rolled paper-thin baklava (a Greek pastry) dough for the remainder of his term in service.

Moral: When you justify (or joystify) too much or not at all, you're in deep trouble.

How much is enough? Too much is no good. A little is okay.

Joystifications can be externalized (told to others), or internalized (told to oneself). There are seven types of joystifications, and here they are:

JOYSTIFICATION CHECKLIST

One: Delayer Joystifications put joy on hold. Here are some of the more common reasons people give for delaying pleasure:

> • "Life will be joyous after I get the kids through college/
> they move out/they get married/they are settled in well-
> paying careers."
> • "I'll start living it up when I get a cellular phone/fax
> machine/computer of my own."

• "Life will be terrific once I get through driving school/ med school/graduate school."

• "Things will be great once I have a job/my own place/my nose fixed/lose twenty pounds."

• "I'll be able to afford to enjoy myself once I get a raise/ strike it rich/win the lottery."

• "The real fun starts when I get married/divorced/ remarried."

• "When I have a baby/a dog/a horse/a motorcycle, life will be complete."

• "I'll start living when we buy our own tent/condo/home."

• "What fun we'll have once we have children/grand-children/no kids around."

• "I'll start to enjoy life again once my mother/husband/ child/parakeet recovers."

• "I'll have time to enjoy myself when I'm thirty/forty/fifty/ when I retire."

Two: Blamer Joystifications hold *others* responsible for an ongoing joylessness. The standard blamer joystification starts:

"How can I enjoy myself when . . .
  • my husband snores?"
  • the people next door have such noisy parties?"
  • my child gets rotten grades?"
  • my wife spends money like a drunken sailor?"
  • my husband doesn't want to go anywhere?"
  • my wife makes more money than I do?"
  • my husband won't clean up after himself?"
  • my children won't listen?"
  • my mother treats me like a baby?"

- my best friend bad-mouths me?"
- my father won't let me drive the car?"
- my neighbors are on drugs?"
- my doctor is retiring?"
- my brother keeps teasing me?"
- my son hasn't called me in a week?"
- my cleaning woman didn't show up?"
- my boss is not fair?"

Three: Self-Diminishing Joystifications undermine joyfulness by eroding self-worth and crushing self-esteem. Self-diminishers bemoan their inadequacies but don't do anything about them. They're quick to point out their shortcomings to excuse their being cheerless.

Self-diminishers are easy to recognize—you'll hear them say:

"There's no way I can really enjoy myself because ...
- my butt is beginning to sag."
- I'm shy/stupid/ugly/fat/skinny/bow-legged/cross-eyed."
- I have nothing to be proud of."
- I'm a failure."
- I can't say no."
- I can't trust men/women."
- My bust is too small/too large."
- I can't hold on to friends."
- I have a terrible head for names and numbers."
- I have no knack for making money."
- I'm a rotten judge of people."
- I'm a computer illiterate."

Four: Complainer Joystifications are a subtle form of

joystification. The implied message is "How can I enjoy myself when I'm dissatisfied with almost everything: my health, marriage, children, job, not to mention the economy, weather, traffic, and the way the government is run?"

Complainers differ from *blamers* in that blamers can name names—the specific individuals or situations responsible for their joylessness. Complainers are more subtle; they are dissatisfied with the world in general and think all right-minded people must feel the same.

A typical complainer will say:

"I can't enjoy myself when . . .
  • there are so many rude people at the theater."
  • the government is run by corrupt politicians."
  • it's impossible to find a doctor who knows what he's doing."
  • the traffic is so bad, it takes the fun out of going anywhere."
  • the movies these days are full of smutty language."
  • you can't buy produce that hasn't been poisoned with insecticides."

Unlike blamers, complainers have got something worthwhile going for them. Complaints can serve a worthwhile purpose. They can get others to modify their behavior; they can get satisfaction from rude clerks; they can vent frustration. Complaining cancer patients have been found to get better medical care—and have a better prognosis—than their meek counterparts.

How much complaining is acceptable? Too much is no good. A little is all right.

Five: Boredom Joystifications are recognizable by such statements as "Life is boring" or "Is that all there is?" Individuals who blame joylessness on boredom are usually suffering an underlying depression, the real reason for their boredom as well as their lack of pleasure in life.

Here are a few things boredsters say:

- "I've tried it all and there's nothing left to do."
- "There are no new frontiers left to conquer."
- "Nothing excites me anymore."
- "Life's a drag."

Six: Self-Begrudging Joystifications. People who begrudge themselves pleasure and joyfulness have a martyr complex. What they're saying—maybe without knowing it—is "See how virtuous I am. I am denying myself the good things in life and that proves I'm a selfless and morally superior person."

Self-begrudgers say, "It's hard to enjoy myself because ...

- I have to save for my old age."
- I just can't spend money on myself."
- I don't want it."
- I don't need it."
- I can get along without it."

Seven: Diminisher Joystifications. When you justify joylessness by comparing yourself favorably to other individuals or groups, you're a diminisher.

The usually unexpressed thought is "I may not enjoy myself as much as you-know-who, but I'm a better person because ...

- he's so busy enjoying himself, he couldn't possibly take care of his responsibilities."

- she's so self-indulgent, she must be ignoring her husband, home, and children."
- he's so hell-bent on pleasure, he's bound to be a failure."
- she behaves like a spoiled, brainless, fun-loving child."
- most New Yorkers, Californians, rock musicians, movie stars, young people, and divorcées are nothing but hedonists."

Don't be too quick to knock hedonists! You may be surprised to learn that you're a hedonist yourself!

If your aim is to seek pleasure and avoid pain, search out intellectual as well as sensual enjoyments, look for opportunities to fill your life with joyous experiences, and believe that happiness is the sum of pleasures, you qualify as a hedonist. That's not all bad.

Hedonists have been given a bad rap. They've been misrepresented by diminishers who mistakenly assume hedonism concentrates on purely physical pleasures. Not so. The true hedonist recognizes the pleasures derived from fame and reputation, from friendship and sympathy, from knowledge and art.

On the other hand, if you believe you should seek pain and avoid the pleasures of the moment, you could be a masochist. If you believe it's sinful to pleasure yourself, perhaps you're a religious fanatic. If you pursue intellectual pleasures but turn up your nose at physical delights, you could be a prude.

If you're not a hedonist, masochist, religious fanatic, or a prude, chances are you're a nice person who would simply like to get more joy out of life.

ONE SMALL STEP TOWARD JOYFULNESS

Are you a joystifier? If you're not sure, ask one or two close friends or family members to read this chapter and then honestly tell you whether you joystify more or less than most people they know.

If you're not up to revealing yourself to others, use this rule of thumb: If you have lots of good reasons for missing out on life's pleasures, chances are you're a joystifier.

RULE FOUR

You Can Talk Yourself into and out of Joylessness

Without love, hatred, joy, or fear,
They led—a kind of—as it were:
Nor wish'd, nor car'd, nor laugh'd, nor cry'd:
And so they liv'd, and so they dy'd.

> "An Epitaph"
> Matthew Prior

4

Say "Adieu, Adiós, Aloha, Arrivederci, Au Revoir, Auf Wiedersehen, Bon Voyage, Bye, Cheerio, Ciao, Farewell, Good Day, Good-bye, Sayonara, Shalom, So Long" to Unhappy Talk

People paint themselves into joyless corners with joystifications (unhappy talk).

It is told that in one of their many conversations, Abdulla, son of Hussein ibn Ali, emir of Mecca, and Thomas Edward Lawrence (better known as Lawrence of Arabia) discussed Arab wives.

Lawrence asked Abdulla, "After having visited with a number of sheikhs I noticed that their many wives were in high spirit, whereas in England where a man is permitted but one wife, she often turns out to be a troublesome shrew. How do you account for the merriment amongst Arab wives?"

"Because it is so written," replied Abdulla. "The Koran states that a wife should—"

"Yes, but how do you manage it?" Lawrence interrupted.

"We choose joyous females," replied Abdulla.

"You hardly see them before marriage and when you do, they're wearing *hejabs* [face covers]," said Lawrence. "For God's sake, how do you manage to choose women who will remain joyful?"

"I can't speak for all families, but we use a clever *fekih,* or as you would say, a marriage intermediary or emissary," explained Abdulla. "After the girl's father grants the *fekih* permission to speak to his daughter, he asks her many questions. He asks her whether she's ever sad. If she answers no, she is lying and would not make a worthy wife."

"That's it!" exclaimed Lawrence.

"Hold your camels," responded Abdulla. "If she answers yes, she's then asked, 'How often are you sad?' If she answers 'frequently,' or 'often,' she's disqualified. If she answers 'seldom' or 'occasionally,' he then asks, 'How do you account for your occasional sadness?' If she blames someone or a life condition or says, 'It's Allah's will,' she is disqualified."

"Then who's left?" asked Lawrence.

"Those few who blame no one for their occasional sadness," said Abdulla as he scooped up two fingers of *baba ghanouj* [dip made with eggplant].

"That doesn't make any bloody sense," said Lawrence. "It would seem that women who are sad on occasion and don't know why would make poor wives indeed."

"You miss the point," Abdulla said with a smile. "Women who don't resort to blame are more joyous than sad and overcome their sadness more quickly."

Lawrence thought for a while, nodded, then belched politely.

*　　*　　*

Abdulla may have stretched the truth a bit We've yet to meet a person who hasn't at some time justified joylessness. But he exhibited down-to-earth ancient wisdom, since confirmed by modern psychology, when he accurately noted that blamers are least joyful and take longer to overcome sadness. Some never do.

As a toddler Lisa B., a late talker, learned to point and whine to get what she wanted: candy at the supermarket, Jell-O for dessert, cotton candy at the zoo. As she grew older without ditching the habit, her father teased, "If you don't stop your whining, we'll skip Disneyland this year and take you to the Napa Valley—'whine' country."

Lisa knew when she had a good thing going: at five she nagged for a two-wheeler with training wheels; at seven for a Barbie doll "completely outfitted." By ten she had added "blaming" to her repertoire.

She blamed teachers/brother/the class bully for low grades; school lunches for her acne; loneliness on her parents for not living in a nicer neighborhood/not sending her to a fancy summer camp/not being able to afford private school.

By the time she reached dating age, Lisa was adept at justifying every setback, disappointment, and frustration by pointing a blaming finger at someone. Her social life, she said, was restricted by her lack of an adequate wardrobe—her father's fault since he didn't earn enough money to outfit her properly. When her SAT scores weren't high enough to gain her admittance to the college of her choice, she blamed her mother for not having arranged for a private tutor. An early marriage that ended in failure would never have taken place if only her parents had made her happier at home. Lisa has since remarried and has two children who, she claims, are keeping her from "making it big" as an Avon Lady. And "if my husband were only more ambitious and tried harder to get ahead, I'd be a much happier person."

JUSTIFYING JOYSTIFICATIONS

Letting go of joystifications requires an understanding of how they keep you mired in joylessness.

When we tell individuals who get little pleasure out of life that they must minimize their delaying, blaming, self-blaming, complaining, and diminishing, here are some of the justifications they come up with:

DELAYERS: *"What's wrong with having something to look forward to?"*

It's fine to have goals, but when future goals are "excuses" for not enjoying yourself in the present, you're bound to be a mostly joyless person.

Since delayers are usually socially unsure or intimidated by the unfamiliar, their I'll-enjoy-myself-tomorrow approach to life, can be a way of avoiding threatening involvements.

BLAMERS: *"Why should I forgive and forget someone who's made me miserable?"*

It's normal to be unable or even unwilling to forgive or forget. It's maladaptive when you become so mired in anger and bitterness that it interferes with your ability to enjoy life fully.

Blamers are usually anxious about their inability to assert themselves effectively, and are either belligerent or passive.

SELF-BLAMERS: *"I'm aware of my limitations, so why kid myself?"*
Knowing your limitations is okay, but using them to justify joylessness is not okay.

When·you keep telling yourself you're too ugly, stupid, lazy, sick, shy, awkward, to be happy or successful, you sentence yourself to lifelong discontent.

Unlike blamers who direct fault-finding and anger at others, self-blamers are angry at themselves and have all but given up hope for happiness. Helplessness and hopelessness compound their problems. They tend to be the most unhappy joystifiers.

COMPLAINERS: *"When I tell somebody my problems I feel better."*
Of course you feel better, but have you noticed that after complaining you feel as discontented as ever?

Aside from eliciting sympathy, complaints turn others off. Worse yet, complaining reminds you of unpleasantness and diminishes your capacity for enjoyment.

If you occasionally need assistance with a problem, simply state your problem without whining. If, however, you're continually beset by problems, you may need professional help.

BOREDSTERS: *"Believe me, I've done it all. There's nothing left to give me a thrill."*
You may think so, especially if you've experienced many things: ridden the Orient Express, summered in Spain, gambled for high stakes at the tables at Vegas, had mad affairs, gone scuba diving, parachuted from a plane, risked your life in pursuit of adventure.

Boredsters, convinced they have tried all possible distractions, often become despondent and depressed.

If, despite all you've experienced, you're left with an is-that-all-there-is? feeling, chances are you've missed out on life's most pleasurable (albeit occasionally painful) ventures. You've some-how avoided committing yourself to anything meaningful—a long-term intimate relationship, a challenging career, or a soul-satisfying leisure-time activity.

SELF-BEGRUDGERS: *"I don't need much,"* or *"I have enough,"* or *"If I don't provide for my old age who will?"* or *"My children need things more than I do,"* or *"Happy-go-lucky people are self-centered and selfish,"* are the sounds of people who have great difficulty parting with money or who are overly sensitive about how they're perceived by others.

If you find it difficult to spend money on yourself, perhaps you fear impoverishment, and have either experienced hard times or were raised by parents anxious about being poor.

If you deny yourself pleasures because you fear being viewed as irresponsible, you've probably been influenced by extremely demanding parents.

Whatever the reason, the only way to break free of your mind-set is to force yourself to be good to yourself. It's better than waking up one day regretting all the things you could have done

(More advice for self-begrudgers and individuals who think they need lots of money to enjoy themselves can be found in Chapter Eight.)

DIMINISHERS: Diminishers joystify their unhappy existence with the pretense that joylessness endows one with moral superiority. Self-begrudgers often resort to diminishing to disguise their resentment of people who manage to enjoy life more than they do.

A typical *diminisher* remark: "I'd have more time to enjoy myself if I were like some other people who don't care if they're neglecting their home and family," or "I could spend money on myself if I were like those selfish types who always think of themselves first," or "I would enjoy more success if I were as ruthless and cold-blooded as some people I know."

If you repeatedly diminish others, face up to the likelihood that it's your envy—not your honesty—that prompts you to belittle their life-styles.

LES MISERABLES

A couple of years ago Sol accepted an invitation to appear on a TV talk show. His assignment—to try his hand at helping four self-proclaimed miserable people.

He was sandwiched between two unhappy women seated to his right and a despondent man and malcontented woman seated to his left. After brief introductions the host asked one of the women to tell Sol what was making her so gloomy.

She reported that her husband hadn't spoken to her in years; that her friends were unsupportive because they were wrapped up in their own problems; that her selfish parents had pushed her into a sorry marriage.

Sol had to admit, her sour and whiny disposition left him less than sympathetic.

He told her, "Your husband, friends, and parents were sending you a message."

"What kind of message?" the host asked.

"To lighten up and stop complaining." Sol suggested she pretend to be happy for a month.

"Everything I told you was true," the guest protested, "and I can't pretend being happy when I'm miserable!"

The host accused Sol of being hostile, and introduced miserable person #2, a real sad sack. He told how he had to work his (bleeping) tail off to keep his unappreciative wife and kids happy, how his boss (bleeped) him out of a raise, that at every turn he gets (bleeped).

Sol asked him, "Have you ever tried giving without getting?" and was accused of being unfriendly. He wasn't getting anywhere so he began praying for a miracle. He thought, *I was told a long time ago that it's all right to pray for miracles—but don't expect them to happen.* However, a miracle did happen when a viewer called in.

The caller identified herself as a fifty-two-year-old happily married woman.

"You wretched people," she began. "Why don't you listen to Dr. Gordon? He's right about all of you, you know.

"Seven years ago I got a divorce and I was miserable. Many of my friends abandoned me, I was lonely, I wasn't getting younger, everything was either sagging or aching, and I complained, boy did I complain.

"Then a friend told me, 'If you want to stop being unhappy, then stop talking about how miserable you are. And instead of sitting home feeling sorry for yourself, put a smile on your face and go out and do something for someone who's worse off than you are.'

"I heard and I listened. I stopped complaining as much as I could, forced myself to smile, and I became a hospital volunteer.

"You would think that being around sick people would make you even more dejected, but I forgot my troubles and found that the other volunteers were a lot of fun to be with.

"One volunteer was a short, fat bald man who became interested in me. At first I didn't pay him any attention, but then we became friends.

"He's now my husband—the best short, fat bald husband in the world."

LETTING GO!

Joystifications, like other addictions, are difficult to shake, and kicking the habit can be as painful as quitting smoking, overeating, or drugs.

How do you let go? *You stop!*

Stop telling yourself, and others, that you'll enjoy yourself later, that other people and situations are to blame for your joylessness, that you can't enjoy yourself because you're worthless. Stop telling yourself and others that life is a drag because you're beset by problems, that there's nothing more to enjoy because you've done it all, that you can't afford enjoyments, and that people who are out to enjoy life to the fullest don't take their responsibilities seriously and probably suffer from a personality defect.

Try *not* talking about your concerns for a few days. Focus instead on other people's interests.

When asked, "How are things?" "How're you doing?" "How do you feel?" respond with a cheerful "Wonderful," "Great," "Terrific." Try "Couldn't be better," even if you have to lie.

The first month or so will be a trial. You'll feel wretched forcing yourself to bite your tongue very time you're about to complain or blame. After all, joystifications are defenses, and when you don't have them to fall back on you feel defenseless, naked.

Squelching the joystifications that creep into your mind is even harder. To stop joy-killing thoughts, tell yourself, "This is stupid. I'm just making myself miserable!" Then distract yourself by concentrating on something pleasant or tantalizing, like an upcoming vacation, a romantic novel, a wonderfully prepared meal with an expensive bottle of wine.

If you're still having trouble controlling your thoughts, try this crutch: buy a stroke counter (a gadget sporting-goods stores sell to help golfers keep track of their strokes) to wear on your wrist. Click it each time you catch yourself making a mental excuse for being miserable. Make a real effort to lower your score each day.

Listening to a subliminal joy-boosting tape is the easiest way to replace joystifications with upbeat self-talk. Joy tapes are available for $12.95 postpaid from HEALTHSAVERS (P.O. Box 683, Herndon, VA 22070).

Letting go is a painful and lonely undertaking, but with persistence it pays off. How?

Since joystifications keep you locked into joylessness, they make it impossible for you to recognize or take advantage of all opportunities for pleasure that come your way.

Even more important: Since it's extremely difficult to face up to and deal with the anxieties that underlie your unhappiness while you're intent on legitimizing joylessness, it's essential that you give up joystifying.

RULE FIVE

To Maximize Joy You Must Minimize Anxiety

If I can stop one Heart from breaking
I shall not live in vain
If I can ease one Life the Aching
Or cool one Pain

Or help one fainting Robin
Unto his Nest again
I shall not live in Vain.

Emily Dickinson
"Life—Part 1"

5

Enter Anxiety—Exit Joy

When we tell people they must minimize their joystifying so they can master the anxieties that keep them from enjoying life more fully, they're ready to do battle.

"Anxious? Of course I'm anxious. Look at all the stress I'm under."

Though we're all subject to stress, have you noticed that some individuals are felled by it, while others thrive on it?

The level of anxiety with which we respond to stress is what separates victors from victims, winners from losers, the joyful from the joyless. Hardy persons with low levels of anxiety are able to shrug off life's stresses, while the anxiety ridden fall prey to stress.

There are two major categories of anxiety: CHANGE ANXIETY and SOCIAL ANXIETY.

CHANGE ANXIETY is the apprehension or fear experienced when facing a threatening or unfamiliar event.

SOCIAL ANXIETY is the distress experienced when facing a person you view as threatening, superior, or disagreeable. It's that deep-in-the-guts sensation—"They're heeeere"—made famous in the movie *Poltergeist.*

Though stress has received top billing as Public Enemy Number One, it's the anxious response to stress that's the real culprit.

How does anxiety interfere with joy?

The more anxious you feel, the more self-involved and resistant to pleasure you become. How much fun can you have at a party when you're concerned with the impression you're making? How much joy is there in redecorating your home when you're worried you might be laid off? Can you take real delight in Roseanne, Cosby, Letterman, when you're "on the outs" with your best friend or hubby? What pleasure is there in reading the latest Danielle Steel, Stephen King, or Frederick Forsyth best seller when a child in college hasn't called in a couple of weeks?

Worse still are the self-destructive ways in which many relieve their anxiety: drugs, food, hyperactivity, sexual promiscuity, gambling, or other risky ventures.

Another common escape mechanism is dreams, which, when properly analyzed, can provide people with useful insight into what's bugging them.

To illustrate how precisely a dream can illuminate the underpinnings of emotionally laden concerns, here's our version of L. Frank Baum's *The Wonderful Wizard of Oz.*

Whether you loved the book or the movie, chances are you thought the tale's message was "You can find happiness in your own backyard."

That's only part of the story. What the tale also reveals is how dreams expose the anxiety-ridden personality of an unhappy little girl.

As Baum tells it, Dorothy, an orphan, lives with her aged aunt and uncle in a one-room farmhouse in Kansas—a grim and joyless place. Only Toto, her dog, makes 'Dorothy laugh and saves her from growing as bleak as her surroundings.

One day along comes a cyclone. Everyone rushes to the storm cellar, but in her frantic search to find Toto, Dorothy is knocked unconscious by flying debris and begins her dream adventure. After dreaming that she has fallen asleep she is awakened by the shock of the tornado-tossed house landing in a beautifully landscaped and vividly colored place.

(Analysis: Dorothy, a ward of cheerless custodians, and with no friendly companion besides Toto, turns to dreams to escape her desolation.)

As Baum's tale continues, a little old woman approaches and says, in a sweet voice, "You are welcome, most noble Sorceress, to the land of the Munchkins. We are so grateful to you for having killed the Wicked Witch of the East, and for setting our people free from bondage." (The house had accidentally landed on the Wicked Witch.) Dorothy is presented with the Wicked Witch's charmed silver shoes and, after being urged to do so, puts them on.

(Analysis: Since she distrusts adults, Dorothy conjures up Munchkins—adults cut down to her size. She secretly despises Aunt Em, whom she blames for her unhappiness. In her dream the house accidentally kills the Wicked Witch, who symbolizes her aunt, and thus satisfies her murderous thoughts. Dorothy craves the attention Uncle Henry pays her aunt, and wearing the Wicked Witch's shoes reveals her desire to take Aunt Em's place.)

Back to the tale: After telling the Munchkins that she is eager to return to her Kansas home, she is directed by them to the Yellow Brick Road, which leads to the Emerald City where Oz, the Great Wizard—and the only one who can help her—resides.

(Analysis: Her request to return to desolate Kansas so soon after her arrival in beautiful Munchkinland, where she's given royal treatment, attests to her guilt-ridden conviction—a result of her upbringing—that there's something wicked about enjoyment.)

On her trip to Oz she meets a Scarecrow, the Tin Woodman, and a Cowardly Lion, who ask to join her on the trip to the Emerald City.

Dorothy invites the Scarecrow along after he reveals that he has no brains, believes that the Wizard can provide them, and admits that the one thing he fears is a lighted match.

She accepts the Tin Woodman after he confesses he has no heart, is counting on the Wizard to furnish one, and admits that the one thing he fears is not being able to love someone.

She takes in the Cowardly Lion after he reveals that he has no courage, expects the Wizard can supply him with some, and acknowledges that the one thing he fears is being afraid.

Dorothy reveals nothing about herself.

(Analysis: The Scarecrow, Tin Woodman, and Cowardly Lion embody Dorothy's underlying inadequacies and fears. In having to resort to dreams and dream symbols, she reveals that she's unable to deal with her anxieties when awake.)

On their journey to Oz, Dorothy talks about Kansas, "and how gray everything was there. . . ." The Scarecrow listens carefully and says, "I cannot understand why you should leave this beautiful country and go back to the dry, gray place you call Kansas."

"That is because you have no brains," snaps a hostile and defensive Dorothy.

With the Wizard's help the Scarecrow gets his brains; the Woodman, his heart; the Lion, his courage; and Dorothy gets to return to Kansas to live with her joyless Aunt Em and Uncle Henry.

(Analysis: Dorothy's anxiety is so overwhelming, she can no longer fully enjoy her escapist dreams. Dorothy's home in Kansas symbolizes unhappiness, but like millions of other Dorothys [and Donalds] she becomes so anxious when confronted by the prospect of change and the necessity of coping with the unfamiliar, she deprives herself of attainable pleasures.)

The classic tale is an example of the way a "normally" anxious person uses dreams. Uncomfortable with people in authority, uptight when confronted by the unfamiliar, envious of anyone more fortunate, unable to do anything to correct a joyless situation, the individual turns to an escapist activity to relieve anxiety.

Are you doing the same?

Do you sometimes become so anxious in social situations or when faced with the unfamiliar that you must turn to tranquilizing food, sleep, drugs, or alcohol to numb your dismay?

When anticipating uncertainty or when you are approached by a stranger, do your hands become cool and clammy? Does your heart race? Do you have difficulty thinking clearly? Does your breathing become shallow? Do you become "antsy"? Do you rush to the phone to call a friend? Do you become ravenous or lose your appetite? Do your shoulder and neck muscles tighten? Do you feel weak in the knees?

If you answered yes to any of the above, you're not alone. There are millions of unfortunate people who fail to enjoy life more fully because they become anxious in specific social situations or when facing change. If you happen to be one of them, take heart. CHANGE ANXIETY and SOCIAL ANXIETY are not incurable conditions. They can be overcome, even in today's highly stressful environment.

The following case of Dot L.—a modern-day Dorothy—should inspire new hope in readers who would like to add more sunshine to their lives.

Here's her account of a typical day:

"When the phone woke me, I started worrying about who could be calling so early—it had to be bad news. After I learned it was just a wrong number, I felt this was not going to be a good day.

"Still unnerved by the call, I lost my appetite for breakfast, dumped the cereal in the sink, gulped down half a cup of coffee, and decided to make up for the missed meal with a big lunch.

"I set off for work and met up with gridlock traffic—the parkway resembled a cement parking lot—but I've learned how to handle commuter stress and settled back to listen to a motivational tape. Only, there was a funny noise coming from under the hood, and it worried me so, I couldn't concentrate on the relaxation message.

"When I arrived at work and heard a staff meeting had been called for one-thirty, at which time we'd get to meet our new boss, my heart sank. I wasn't prepared for the meeting, hadn't dressed impressively, and if I took time to shop for a new outfit, would have to skip lunch. I worried so over which to do—eat or shop—I couldn't concentrate on my work, made one goof after another, and had to give up my lunch hour to make up.

"Then came the meeting, which went so much better than feared—the new boss assured us there would be no policy changes, and that his door was open to anyone with suggestions on how to improve working conditions—I kicked myself for having become so upset.

"During my afternoon coffee break I was so famished, I chomped down two candy bars and told my friend Susan, 'There goes my diet.'

"She said, 'Lighten up. Come to the square dance with me tonight.'

"When I told her I was exhausted from the day's mishaps, she told me my only trouble was I don't have enough fun. Ha!

"Just then a good-looking stranger came into the employee lounge. He introduced himself as one of the new employees, and he and Susan got into a lively conversation, but since I couldn't figure out whether he was a bigwig or not, I decided to play it safe and hardly said a word.

" 'How about an after-work drink?' he asked Susan. 'Your quiet friend can come along'—he included me in the invitation.

"Susan gave me an encouraging let's-do-it look, but I begged off.

"It was a hectic day and I was zonked, so I told her, 'I'm really not dressed for any evening activities, and I think I'll just head home and try to get a decent night's sleep. Thanks all the same.'

"On the drive home I thought about my day. I felt I had done the right thing in turning down an evening out that could turn into a disaster. I could just picture everyone at the office laughing at me if the new guy turned out to be married, or a letch.

"But why do I fell so heavy-hearted—and so damn tired?"

Dot's day typifies that of many women and men. Even when she's having fun, it's dampened by an underlying pervasive anxiety, and as a consequence she can't completely "let go."

Dot was referred to Sol by a physician who couldn't find anything physically wrong to account for her chronic fatigue.

After one session it was clear that she was both bored and depressed, common bedfellows of fatigue. It has been esti-mated that over half of all adult Americans—close to sixty million people—are chronically fatigued because they're bored. Boredom causes depression, and when you are depressed, body functions slow up, you have difficulty achieving restful sleep, you lose your appetite or overeat—all of which cause you to become increasingly fatigued.

When people complain, "I'm bored to death," or "I'm dead tired," they're not exaggerating. Boredom and fatigue are real killers.

How can a pretty woman like Dot, who seemingly had every-thing going for her, be bored? She was afraid to face life. She was fearful of specific people, became anxious in the presence of authorities, was uneasy with men, uptight at gatherings, and nervous when meeting strangers. Dot suffered from SOCIAL ANXIETY, and more.

She was equally fearful of the unfamiliar, afraid of becoming involved in new experiences. On two occasions she *almost* married. She's turned down two lucrative job offers, because she feared she wouldn't feel comfortable ·in a new work environment. She's vacationed at the same Florida resort since she graduated school seven years ago, and continues to live in the same apartment she rented in 1982, despite the fact that she can afford better and the neighborhood is continually deteriorating. Dot is also afraid of change—a victim of CHANGE ANXIETY.

Since SOCIAL ANXIETY and CHANGE ANXIETY are the two culprits that cut people off from new relationships and exciting experiences, they are the major contributors to boredom, depression, fatigue—and joylessness.

Dot had to conquer her anxieties before she could free herself from boredom and fatigue and, with help, was able to do so. She triumphed over SOCIAL ANXIETY with Mitzvah Therapy (Chapter 6); and prevailed over CHANGE ANXIETY with Chutzpah Therapy (Chapter 7). After three months she was a changed woman—energetic, enthusiastic, joyful, and ready to take on the world.

Dot was an admittedly extreme case. Not everyone who's anxious is also bored and fatigued. But one thing is for sure—all anxiety-ridden people feel they're missing out on life's pleasures.

It shouldn't take you any longer than Dot to enjoy significant positive changes, if you will follow the suggestions in this book. We can't promise overnight success, but we can guarantee you will, without question, stop attainable pleasures from slip-sliding away.

One note of caution: You're going to have to work at it. Attaining a more joyful life is no simple matter, despite what some pop psychologists would have you believe. The simplistic Simple-Simon-sez-do-this-do-that approach rarely works.

Thousands of how-to books and articles have misled readers into believing that happiness is just around the corner, easily arrived at by following such simplistic stop-start directives as: *Stop* watching so much TV; *start* finding ways to entertain yourself; *stop* waiting for exciting things to happen; *start* thinking positively; *stop* focusing on obstacles.

Great advice—if only readers were also advised how to reduce the anxieties that keep them from following such guidelines.

To attain a more joyful life you must first deal with the anxieties that stand in your way, and for starters, you must admit they exist.

Go ahead, admit that you become anxious when ...

- faced with unpredictable change
- among strangers
- confronted with an unfamiliar task
- things don't go right
- you're alone
- you're in a strange city
- you receive official-looking mail
- your spouse won't talk to you
- you have to wait in line
- your car acts up

- you believe someone's mad at you
- you feel that life is passing you by.

If none of the above applies to you, you're indeed a very fortunate person. If, however, you occasionally suffer feelings of boredom, mild depression, or unexplainable tiredness, chances are you're more anxious—and joyless—than you're willing to admit.

RULE SIX

Help Yourself to Happiness by Bringing Joy to Others

Merlin motioned, "Come to the edge."
But they held back and said, "It's dangerous."
He beckoned, "Come to the edge."
And they said, "We may fall."
Then he commanded, "Come to the edge!"
So, they went to the edge and he pushed them . . .
And they flew.

Adapted from the works of
Guillaume Apollinaire

6

"Mitzvahs"

Experience the Joy of Unconditional Giving

Contemporary definition of a "mitzvah": Hebrew word for a blessing received when a kindness is extended without fanfare and without expecting anything in return.

HEAVEN IS LIKE BOCA RATON, BUT PARADISE IS LIKE PALM BEACH

When virtuous Fred Danforth died, he was sure he qualified for paradise but was turned down when the admitting angel learned he was totally sinless.

"But I don't understand. I've lived a righteous life!" Fred protested.

"Let me explain," said the angel. "While it's true that paradise is set aside for exemplary people, not one of them is completely without sin, and it just wouldn't be fair to subject them to the discomfort of having someone around who's never transgressed."

"Fair! Do you think *I'm* being treated fairly?" Fred pleaded.

"Tell you what I'm going to do," said the angel. "You go back to earth and commit one sin within twenty-four hours and I'll reconsider your case."

"But I don't know how to sin."

"Try adultery," suggested the angel.

Fred left, and twelve hours later returned with a big, fat, self-satisfied grin.

"Well, what happened?" asked the angel.

Fred was too embarrassed to speak.

"You gotta tell me to get in," said the angel.

"Well," said Fred, "I met this ugly old woman who had been a widow for thirty years—"

"Stop right there," the angel interrupted. "You blew it. Disqualified!"

"But I sinned!" said Fred.

"That was no sin," the angel whispered. "That was a mitzvah."

Of course, the angel was kidding. He knew that even if Fred's sin was a blessing in disguise, he had passed the test and was entitled to enter paradise.

The angel wouldn't have received his B.A. (Bachelor of Angels degree) if he didn't know that mitzvah givers are entitled to two payoffs: the satisfaction derived from giving, and salvation. He also knew that those who give expecting anything additional are often rewarded with disappointment, distrust, anger, and social anxiety.

When Sol explained all this to one unhappy mother who had

come to see him, she asked, "Do you mean to tell me that after giving my daughter the best years of my life, sacrificing my chances for a career, caring for her when she was sick, scrimping so that she could have music lessons and a college education, that I *shouldn't* expect her to love, respect, and take care of me in my old age? Brother, you're crazy!"

Sol assured her that he was sane and serious and continued, "If you're as religious as you say you are, then you should know that God loves those who give ungrudgingly and never boast of their generosity. It doesn't count as a good deed if you give expecting anything in return."

She looked at him as if he'd taken leave of his senses and said, "You must be kidding. Do you mean to tell me that when I give to charity I can't take a deduction?"

"If you take a deduction," he told her, "it's no longer a mitzvah."

She said, "Talking to you is like talking to a wall," and walked off in a huff.

THE MITZVAH PUZZLE

People find the mitzvah concept perplexing.

"It's unrealistic," they reason. "How can anyone, other than saints and screwballs, give without expecting something in return?"

One skeptic said, "I'd like to meet the person who does favors, gives gifts, loans money, extends invitations, without expecting to be repaid by equally good treatment."

"You miss the point," Sol told him. "There are situations, such as working overtime, when it's appropriate to expect to be financially rewarded. On the other hand, there's no mitzvah if you're motivated to give in hopes of getting something back. Moreover, social relationships are often a disaster when either party has a hidden tit-for-tat agenda. There's no blessing and no real love when you're making a secret unilateral deal."

Nardus D. is an accredited and recognized Dutch clairvoyant, world famous for his psychic accuracy.

One day his friend Van came to him for a reading. "Tell me what's in store for my wife, Katrina, and me. Our marriage isn't working out. She doesn't appreciate anything I do and takes advantage of me."

Nardus—who's not above improvising the future to help people, particularly friends—tranced, spun his wand, and peered into his crystal ball.

"No problem," Nardus assured Van. "In about a year you'll be out of the marriage, free of Katrina."

"I'm going to leave her?" Van asked.

"No, she's going to leave you," Nardus said sadly. "Katrina doesn't know it, but she has a fatal disease and won't live past her next birthday."

Van was shocked. "Are you sure?"

Nardus was insulted. "Positive! I'm never wrong."

More than a year passed before Van and Nardus met again at the skate-sharpening stand.

"How goes it?" asked Nardus.

"We sit down and talk, yes?"

Nardus agreed and they adjourned to a nearby coffee shop.

"Well, how goes it?" Nardus asked again.

"Fine, couldn't be better. Katrina and I are gloriously happy. She's turned into a wonderful wife again and every day is like a honeymoon."

Nardus smiled and nodded wisely.

"You're not surprised to find out you were wrong?" Van asked. "You said she'd be dead by now, and instead she's not only healthy, she's pregnant, and the doctors say she's in perfect condition."

"So I lied a little." Nardus shrugged. "Sometimes I have to predict the worst to bring about the best."

This story gets mixed responses. Despite the outcome some are appalled by the deception. Some applaud Nardus's cleverness. Others say they get the message—that Van's marriage became blissful once he began treating her nicely without expecting anything in return because he believed she was going to die. And still others say that the story is not relevant—that it was a life-and-death situation and doesn't relate to everyday giving.

Whatever the response, we advise people who find it difficult to give without expecting something in return to tell themselves when giving, "I expect something back, but if I don't get it I won't feel bad." Half a mitzvah is better than none!

NO-STRINGS-ATTACHED GIVING: THE KEY TO OVERCOMING SOCIAL ANXIETY

The idea that mitzvahs—helping others without expecting anything in return—can reduce social anxiety and free people from timidity, shyness, and loneliness is difficult to grasp, and the question we're most often asked is "How?"

Have you noticed that the most socially adept person you know exudes trust, warmth, and love? Makes you feel important? Is sincerely concerned about your welfare? Talks to your interests? Gives from the heart and seems to expect nothing in return? Is fun to be with?

Have you noticed that the most socially anxious person you know is distrustful, guarded, and narcissistic? Is either close-mouthed or talks mostly about his or her concerns? Is insensitive to your interests? Gives grudgingly and on a strict quid-pro-quo basis? Is a drag to be with?

THE BOTTOM LINE DIFFERENCE BETWEEN THE SOCIALLY ADEPT AND THE SOCIALLY ANXIOUS IS A MATTER OF TRUST

At some time in our lives all of us are severely disappointed by someone we've trusted, and the results are often devastating. People unable to withstand such disappointments become distrustful, withdrawn, cynical, pessimistic—and socially anxious.

Those fortunates able to weather such disappointments maintain their trust, openness, positiveness, optimism—and sociability.

How does a distrusting person regain trust and become more socially adept?

By reversing course. By doing the reverse of what he/she is currently doing.

By giving openly and freely instead of giving and expecting something in return. By giving of oneself and time. By becoming a kinder, more thoughtful, more gentle person.

How does unconditional giving beget trust? The act itself necessitates trust and with every succeeding act trust builds.

OTHER MITZVAH PAYOFFS

• The more you focus on making others happy, the less

self-focused you'll become and the more cheerful you'll
be.
• The more freely you give of yourself, the more intimate
and satisfying your relationships will be.
• The more magnanimous you become, the more autono-
mous you'll feel and the more inner joy you'll experience.

Clients involved in mitzvah therapy report all the aforementioned payoffs and are particularly overwhelmed by the inner
joy they experience. After less than two weeks of therapy Emily
L., a thirty-four-year-old single, expressed her feelings this way:
"When I started this mitzvah thing I would have bet that it
wouldn't work, but I figured what the hell, I'll give it a try. I
started by simply being more helpful to everyone at the office. I
then invited a neighbor who had been recently widowed over
for dinner. I complimented a couple of store clerks. I spent the
first weekend on my own, catching up on cleaning and stuff,
and I wasn't lonely. I felt different—like I was a somebody.
"The following week the office seemed to be a much friend-
lier place. We had a rush job and I had to work overtime, but I
didn't complain. Then a strange thing happened. One of the
guys I've had my eye on for months invited me out to dinner.
We hit it off great and for the first time I wasn't uptight on a
first date. We're seeing each other next weekend and I'm
euphoric. I haven't felt this way in a long, long time."
Emily's reporting feeling like a "somebody" is particularly
significant. Others report an "unexplained feeling of release"
or "inner joy."
All these experiences can best be explained as a newfound
sense of control. When individuals start giving unconditionally,
they start feeling more mature, more in charge, more indepen-

dent. It's as if they're saying good-bye to the dependent, demanding, unhappy child within them and discovering that they're adults—"somebodies."

To more clearly explain the underlying motivations and consequences of conditional giving, here's a story that came from a loneliness workshop.

Martha was an impressionable only child, acutely sensitive to her adult-dominated environment. By nature a pleaser, she grew up intent on earning approval, since her parents—one a lawyer, the other a successful businessman—set high standards and were not easily satisfied. At home she did everything she could think of to win parental favor—was obedient, volunteered to run errands, did the dishes, walked the dog without being asked, made dinner when her mother had to work late. At school she struggled to make straight A's, excel at sports, be a model student.

Try as she might Martha never got the love, attention, and applause she craved. As a teenager she turned to strangers to get what she couldn't get at home. She tried to buy friends by sharing her expensive clothes, giving away records, books, rock-concert tickets, paying for treats, but her friendships were short-lived. When a friend took up with someone else, Martha regarded it as a sign of disloyalty, became furious, then would sulk. After a while she would try again—only to be disappointed. Over time Martha grew increasingly distrustful.

A therapist told this story to a loneliness group workshop and invited comments. One was particularly poignant.

"That was me," said a pretty girl tearfully. "My mother liked my little brother more, and no matter how hard I tried to please her, she still treated him better. I did the same thing with friends and it didn't work."

"So?" the therapist asked.

"So what can a kid do?" she replied. "Martha was stuck. She couldn't leave home or attend a workshop!"

The group laughed.

"But you're no longer children," he told them. "Yet many of you are doing what little Martha did. You are conditional givers—you have difficulty giving without expecting something in return.

"Conditional giving helped get you into this loneliness mess and unconditional giving can help get you out."

Why do people give conditionally?

Because somewhere down the line they have felt emotionally shortchanged and have decided the way to get the stroking they long for is to buy affection. When their efforts fall short—when people fail to respond as anticipated—they become increasingly frustrated, cynical, and distrustful.

How much distrust is okay? A little is all right. Too much is no good.

Distrust discourages new relationships, wrecks old ones. Hundreds of marriage counselors, frustrated in their attempts to minimize distrust between couples, have become divorce counselors.

In the seventies New Age psychologists tried to encourage trust with a "fall-back" exercise. Individuals in group therapy were instructed to turn their back to the person standing behind them, then fall back, trusting that individual to catch them. Needless to say, the exercise failed to inspire trust, but did provide some entertainment.

Next came assertiveness training, wherein socially anxious people were taught to be brazen. Most trainees either couldn't follow through or became offensively hostile. Assertiveness training has gone the way of the fall-back exercise.

Behaviorists who've wrestled with social anxiety, distrust, low self-esteem, and similar problems for years without success could have found the answer in mitzvah therapy.

Mitzvahs encourage trust, and the more trustful you become, the less socially anxious you'll be. . . . It's that simple.

Though mitzvahs are no shortcut to becoming more trustful, they increase trust in much less time than it takes to become distrustful. The transition from overly distrustful to cautious is not easy ... but it's oh, so rewarding!

To ease the changeover to *unconditional* giving, start by forgiving individuals who triggered your distrust.

TRY FORGIVING BEFORE GIVING

If you can find it in your heart to *forgive* the person or persons who initially disappointed you—usually a parent, older relative, sibling, sometimes a spouse—you will release much of the pent-up anger and distrust that prevent you from giving more freely.

If face-to-face forgiving is difficult or impossible, use your imagination. Here's how:

In your mind's eye, picture that person seated opposite you and say something like this: "I was really hurt and angered by your behavior. It's not important whether you deliberately or unconsciously meant to cause me pain. What is important is that I forgive you.

"_____(person's name), I release you from blame and myself from anger."

If you're uncomfortable with the above, then write a letter saying basically the same thing. You don't have to mail it.

Forgiving (before giving) eases mitzvah giving.

ONE MORE TIME

How do mitzvahs make life more joyful?

- Repeated mitzvahs or unconditional giving encourages and bolsters trust.
- The less distrustful, suspicious, and cynical you become, the less timid or belligerent, the more open and self-revealing you'll be in social settings.
- The less socially anxious you are, the more pleasant and attractive you'll become.
- The more pleasant and attractive, the more friends you'll make—and keep.
- The more friends you have, the stronger your social network and the more joyful you'll be.

MITZVAH SUGGESTIONS

In addition to run-of-the-mill mitzvahs like visiting a sick friend and bringing her some chicken soup; helping an aged or impaired person get to the doctor; offering to shop for a neighbor whose child or spouse is sick; volunteering to care for children when their parents must visit someone in the hospital; taking time to share your expertise with a younger or inexperienced co-worker; doing volunteer work in a hospital, school, or for a charity; raising money or collecting food for some destitute family—here are some creative mitzvahs:

- If you're proficient in a specific sport or activity, invite a novice to be your bridge, tennis, golf, dance, or bowling partner.

• Invite a neighbor whose family lives far away to share your holiday dinner, come to your family picnic, attend a family celebration.

• Compliment a waitress, mailman, supermarket checker, bag boy, librarian on his or her attractiveness, sense of humor, patience, efficiency, friendliness.

• Say something kind to someone you never expect to see again.

• Feed a stray cat, put feed out for birds, feed a stranger's expired parking meter.

• Volunteer to teach an illiterate to read, newcomers to speak English, tutor a latchkey kid in his worst school subject.

• Take time to run an errand for a busy friend, read to a sight-impaired senior citizen, advise a newly arrived neighbor of the best places to shop.

• Give small just-for-being-you gifts to people you like— relatives, friends, neighbors, and store clerks.

NOTE: None of the above mitzvahs involves spending a lot of money. Giving of yourself—your time, energy, skill, thoughtfulness, humanity—is more of a mitzvah than simply donating money to some charity or panhandler. Real mitzvahs are gifts from the heart rather than the pocketbook.

BEYOND MITZVAHS

While mitzvahs pave the way to lasting and more joyful relationships, here are a few guidelines to help you reach those goals more quickly:

- DON'T rely on any one person—friend or spouse—to fill most of your emotional needs.
- DO find absorbing creative activities to become involved in when you're alone.
- DON'T expect your boss to be vocally appreciative. Be satisfied with other rewards—a raise, promotion, a job well done, friends made at work.
- DO be an active participant instead of a passive spectator.
- DON'T keep your partner in the dark about your sexual desires and needs.
- DO avoid depressing individuals.
- DON'T blame yourself or someone else when you fail to hit it off. Some personalities clash.
- DO learn to overlook minor indiscretions.
- DON'T be a slave to other people's expectations.
- DO smile more.
- DON'T refute compliments.
- DO say "I love you" more often.

Is it possible to overdo mitzvahs?

Of course. You can make yourself miserable trying to please everybody.

Along these lines, the story of a mule called Hiney.

Things weren't going well for a Swiss farmer, who decided to sell his mule, Hiney—so he and his grandson set forth to the city where the animal would be sold.

On the way a woman shouted, "Fools! Why are you walking when you have a mule and can ride?" They decided she had a point and mounted the mule.

Farther down the road a herdsman berated them. "With both of you riding, that mule will collapse of exhaustion!" Hearing this the grandfather dismounted.

Next a farmer spied them and shouted, "You selfish lad, making your grandfather walk while you ride! Aren't you ashamed?" The boy jumped off and urged his grandfather back on.

As they neared the city, a milkmaid called out, "That poor mule looks as if he is going to drop dead. Why don't you carry him for a while?"

Thinking she had a point, the grandfather dismounted, hoisted the mule onto his back, and dragged Hiney down the road—but as they crossed a bridge, he lost his footing, dropped the mule into the river, and the poor animal drowned.

Moral: If you try to please everyone, you'll wind up losing your Hiney.

To Conquer Fear You Must Feign Courage

*Come, fill the Cup, and in the fire of
    Spring
Your Winter-garment of Repentance
    fling:
  The Bird of Time has but a little way
To flutter—and the Bird is on the
    Wing.*

*Ah, make the most of what we yet may
    spend,
Before we too into Dust descend;
  Dust into Dust, and under Dust, to
    lie,
Sans Wine, sans Song, sans Singer, and
    —sans End!*

The Rubáiyát of Omar Khayyám
—Edward Fitzgerald

7

Tackle the Unknown with "Chutzpah"

Most everybody becomes anxious when confronted by some sort of change. Some find a change in residence particularly threatening; others find parenthood menacing; while still others dread a job, health, financial, diet, or life-style change. Some view change as such a menace, they can't even handle a change for the better.

But one thing is for sure—those least threatened by change and most joyous bank on **CHUTZPAH** (the Hebrew word for audacity, boldness, brashness, cheek, courage, grit, guts, moxie, pluck, and spunk) to see them through.

How much chutzpah do you need?

Too much is offensive. Too little is ineffective.

As Union forces advanced toward Gettysburg, Toothloose Lautrec, a balloonist, approached his captain and requested a weekend pass.

"Are you crazy?" the captain barked. "We're fighting for survival!"

"It's very important that I get back to Intercourse," Toothloose said matter-of-factly. "I have a dry goods store there and this weekend I'm running a big sale. If I'm not present, my help will steal me blind."

The captain was dumbfounded and said to himself, "Either this guy has flipped his lid or he has more chutzpah than Grant. Whatever the case—one thing is for sure—I need him to man that balloon. We must know the disposition of Confederate forces." He stalled for time.

"Tell you what, Lautrec, if you do something heroic, you can have your weekend pass."

"Like what?" asked Toothloose.

"Like capturing a Confederate balloon," responded the captain.

"Okay," said Toothloose, who then hopped into his gondola, rose into the air, and disappeared from sight.

He returned forty-five minutes later with a Confederate balloon. "Voilà, here's your balloon, as requested. Now can I have my weekend pass?"

"Damn," said the befuddled captain, "a deal is a deal. But tell me, Lautrec, how did you do it?"

"Piece of pie," Toothloose explained. "I flew till I saw this Confederate balloon. Then I hollered, 'How would you all like to have a weekend pass?' After I explained the deal, I climbed into the Reb's gondola and he climbed into mine—and here I am!"

Most of us don't have the chutzpah of a Lautrec, but why are some blessed with the guts to tough it out while others succumb to their fears?

When some potentially threatening happening looms, the

timid may agonize for weeks or months—mentally replaying a laundry list of tragic scenarios and unpleasant outcomes.

Anticipatory anxiety may be the most prevalent and insidious of all joy killers. How can you enjoy yourself when you're constantly apprehensive about some impending event—a marriage or divorce, parenthood or children leaving home, a promotion or layoff, a move to a new city or your best friend's moving far away, what your annual medical checkup might reveal, how your tax return will fare under the new IRS rules, next week's sales meeting, next year's college entrance exam, facing retirement ten years from now?

Worriers are often procrastinators as well and compound their anxiety with guilt for avoiding facing the inevitable. And when a dreaded transition finally catches up with them, they're so uptight that it takes them longer to make the change.

Worst of all, should their fears prove ill-founded, hand wringers somehow find something else to worry about and go through life missing out on many pleasures.

There are others who forgo pleasures well within reach because of fear of the unknown. They'll bypass activities they've longed to participate in—sailing, flying, skiing, tennis, scuba diving, square dancing, painting, playing the piano, learning a foreign language—for fear they'll prove incompetent or look foolish. Many don't face up to how much pleasure they've missed until years later, when they bemoan what might have been.

If any of the above sounds familiar, you have our sympathy, but take heart, you can become less fearful.

While most of us don't have a Merlin or some other "pushy" person to give us a shove when we lack chutzpah, we *can* evolve into spunky go-getters.

Scores of initially timid individuals who have blossomed into courageous and self-confident men and women have revealed the secrets of their metamorphosis—PRETENDING and VISUALIZING.

THE POWER OF PRETENDING AND VISUALIZING

Eleanor Roosevelt, a shy and reserved woman, had been careful to maintain a low profile during the twenty-three years her husband was a state senator, assistant secretary of the navy, and governor of New York.

But when FDR was elected President, Eleanor became fearful that she would no longer be able to avoid the spotlight—that the public would discover how awkward and gawky she was.

She revealed her apprehension to a close friend who told her, "You're probably right—you won't be able to hide anymore. But have you ever stopped to think that as the President's wife you're like the queen of the United States?

"Eleanor, do me a favor. Visualize a beautiful crown sitting atop your royal head and when you make your entrance at the inaugural ball, pretend you're a monarch and all the people there are your subjects."

Eleanor agreed to give it a try and discovered what many in similar circumstances have learned—"To *make it*, you must sometimes *fake it*!"

There's no doubt that her friend's invaluable advice helped Eleanor Roosevelt go on to create a new role in the White House for the First Lady of the land and to lead public opinion polls for years as the most admired woman in the world.

However, probably even more important to Mrs. Roosevelt was her ability to enjoy life more fully.

A SHORT PSYCHOLOGY LESSON

We're all subject to the demands of *two* alter egos—a DON'T ego and a DO ego. One prompts us to play it safe, the other to take risks.

Chutzpah-energized persons heed their DO egos more than their DON'T egos. People who are DO ego-oriented enjoy life more than people who are DON'T ego-oriented. End of lesson.

If for years you've been playing it safe, you can activate a dormant DO ego by pretending you're someone courageous when confronted by a threatening change or a tempting activity you're too timid to tackle.

Whether you're successful or not, merely trying will increase your chutzpah. Successes, on the other hand, will increase your self-confidence.

The key is to keep trying, for in so doing you're bound to become more courageous and self-confident and more willing to tackle life's many challenges.

Bolster your courage and build your self-confidence by starting with minimally threatening situations. For example:

- If you've been vacationing at the same place for years, pretend you're a travel agent assigned to accompany clients to a resort you've never visited, and imagine going there to investigate its recreational possibilities.
- Plan an out-of-the-ordinary dinner party, pretending you're Julia Child or Craig Claiborne. Serve up an exotic dessert you've never dared before (check Chapter 12 for some luscious concoctions) and visualize your guests raving and begging for the recipe.
- Next time you have to return merchandise, imagine

you're Ralph Nader.... Then, while pretending you're a spokesperson for a consumer advocacy group, ask to see the manager.
• If you feel out of place shopping at pricey stores, you can sharpen your pretending and visualizing skills by visiting luxury car showrooms. Pretend you're wealthy and visualize impressing salespersons. Do the same thing at the ritziest jewelry or dress shops in town. Polishing your pretending and visualizing skills will help you develop the chutzpah you need to build self-confidence.

Keep practicing until you get the hang of it. Stay on the lookout for chances to rehearse. Persistent visualizing and pretending will help you develop the chutzpah to face more threatening real-life circumstances.
For example:

• When apprehensive about moving to a new locale, pretend you're a courageous pioneer settling the West or a bold immigrant taking up residence in a strange land.
• When faced with an impending career change, bolster your confidence by pretending you're Donald Trump pulling off a big deal.
• When scheduled for major surgery, expect a quick recovery and imagine yourself a much healthier and more energetic person.

Reinforce your self-confidence by celebrating victories. Each time you are able to "pretend away" anxieties, have a "kvellabration" (the Yiddish word for expressing pride is *kvell,* and *kvellabration* is the word we've coined to describe a celebration of an accomplishment you're proud of). Whatever you call it, take pride in your achievement by commemorating the event.

This may all sound frivolous, but it isn't. Science is uncovering the awesome power of guided imagery.

Researchers have found that the appropriate mental images can stimulate immune systems and accelerate cancer remission.

For years hypnotherapists have used visualization techniques to help people quit smoking, lose weight, and rid themselves of warts.

Top athletes use guided imagery to break sports records.

ADDITIONAL SUGGESTIONS

• DO bone up on as much information as possible before making a move. Plan ahead instead of worrying ahead.

• DON'T push your boss for a raise unless you have some seniority.

• DO buoy up your spirits with such uplifting tunes as "I Whistle a Happy Tune," "Singin' in the Rain," "Zip-A-Dee Doo-Dah," "A-Cent-Tchu-Ate the Positive."

• DON'T procrastinate. Schedule work you enjoy most for the end of the day. Set deadlines and put yourself on the spot by committing your intentions to others.

Dr. Albert Ellis,* founder of the Institute for Rational-Emotive Therapy, has written awareness-raising lyrics for a number of well-known tunes. "Oh, How I Hate to Get Up and Get Going!" is particularly appropriate for procrastinators.

---

*We are both fans of Albert Ellis. We recommend his book *How To Stubbornly Refuse to Make Yourself Miserable About Anything—Yes Anything!*

(To be sung to the tune of Irving Berlin's "Oh, How I Hate to Get Up in the Morning.")

> Oh, how I hate to get up and get going!
> Oh, how I love to procrastinate!
> For the hardest thing I know
> Is to hear the whistle blow,
> "You gotta get on, you gotta get on,
> You gotta get on and stop slowing!"
>
> Someday, I promise that I will get going—
> Someday, but never, of course, today!
> I think I'll still procrastinate
> And always get my ass in late,
> And piss the rest of my life away!

• DO take time to consider anxiety-provoking suggestions, offers, and invitations.
• DON'T consider yourself a failure when you fail. Failing at something doesn't make YOU a failure. Failure is an event, not a person!

ONE MORE TIME

How does pretending and visualizing make life more joyful?

• When you pretend you're someone courageous, you're inspired to be courageous.
• When you visualize being courageous, you're motivated to follow through.
• Whether successful or not, you develop chutzpah.

• The more successes you experience, the more self-confident you become.

• The more chutzpah you develop and the more self-confident you become, the less threatened by change and challenging activities you'll be.

• The less fearful you become, the more you'll enjoy life. Enough said.

It's Not How Well Money Is Saved, but How Well It's Spent, that Determines Joyfulness

You're gonna take that ocean trip,
No matter come what may,
You've got your reservations but,
you just can't get away.

Next year for sure you'll see the world
you'll really get around,
BUT HOW FAR CAN YOU TRAVEL
WHEN YOU'RE SIX FEET UNDERGROUND?

ENJOY YOURSELF,
it's later than you think;
ENJOY YOURSELF,
while you're still in the pink.

The years go by
as quickly as a wink,
ENJOY YOURSELF, ENJOY YOURSELF,
it's later than you think.

You're later than you think.

"Enjoy Yourself"
Words by Herb Magidson
Music by Carl Sigman
Copyright by Magidson Music Co., Inc.

8

About Money

Disclosing details about your financial status—your salary, how much you owe, your credit rating—may well be the last conversational taboo.

Most people would reveal the most intimate details of their sex lives before giving an honest answer to how much they're worth. They'll admit to impotence before confessing they earn less than their neighbors!

Nevertheless, people unabashedly claim poverty to excuse a joyless life-style. When you ask people, "Are you having fun?" or "Are you really enjoying yourself?" a frequent response is "It takes more money than I've got."

There's no question that money and fun are interrelated—but not as tightly linked as most people maintain.

For starters, people play some strange games with money.

* * *

Herman and Fritz, two Berlin gemologists, had been friends for years.

During one of their frequent lunch meetings Herman announced his engagement—and having admired a diamond in Fritz's collection, asked whether he could purchase it so that he could have it set in an engagement ring.

A deal was struck and Herman bought the diamond for 2,200 marks.

A week later Herman informed Fritz that the engagement was off. Though Fritz expressed his sympathy, he saw the breakup as an opportunity to buy back his diamond. Herman was hard-nosed and wouldn't part with the gem for a mark less than 3,000. Fritz paid the price.

The following week Herman told Fritz that the engagement was on again and asked whether he would consider reselling the diamond. Fritz refused.

After some pleading Fritz agreed to sell, but only for a rock-bottom price of 3,450 marks. "So be it," said Herman.

At their next weekly meeting Fritz told Herman that he had bad news—that when he told his wife that he had sold the diamond she hit the ceiling because he had promised to have it mounted in a brooch as a tenth-anniversary gift. Fritz assured his wife he could buy back the diamond.

Only after Fritz broke down and cried did Herman agree to part with the diamond. His price? 4,250 marks. Fritz bit his lip and agreed.

A few days later Fritz informed Herman that his wife had changed her mind and wanted diamond earrings instead.

"Good," said Herman. "Now I can use it for the engagement ring after all."

"I'm sorry to tell you this," responded Fritz, "but I sold it to Adolf, the tailor."

"You sold it?" screamed Herman. "You fool—how could you sell it to someone else when for weeks, you and I are making a good living from that diamond!"

This anecdote illustrates the games people play with money— yet despite the fact that Herman and Fritz play the same money games in business, their "money personalities" differ.

Fritz is a "self-begrudger" and finds it extremely difficult to spend money on himself. His mother, who had experienced hard times and feared "ending up in the poorhouse," instilled in him the notion that poverty is always "lurking round the corner" and that it is noble to save.

Fritz is so tightfisted about money that he can't fully enjoy such minor delights as a good play, dinner out at a gourmet restaurant, or wearing a fine suit.

His anxiety and cautiousness extend beyond expenditures. He is so fearful of change that he misses out on such major pleasures as parenthood, a move to a more comfortable home, or a luxury cruise.

Fritz's insecurity and low self-confidence underlie his frugality and his joylessness.

Have you ever noticed that employees who are unsure of their ability or skill invariably turn to penny-pinching ways to save their company money in hopes of holding on to their job?

In contrast Herman is self-indulgent, and although he has no problem spending money, he's often in debt.

His suspicious and cynical nature is the basis for his over-spending. He has a great deal of difficulty sustaining intimate relationships, and as a consequence is often lonely and bored and turns to extravagant purchases and escapist activities for short-term relief—newfangled electronic gadgetry, the latest car model, exotic vacations.

The bottom line: Underlying both Fritz's and Herman's abnormal spending behavior are those two villains—change anxiety and social anxiety. Like so many of us who wish to enjoy life more fully, Fritz must overcome the anxieties that keep him from exploring and taking chances. Herman must overcome his fear of intimacy and commitment.

Fritz must develop the chutzpah necessary to build his self-confidence. People with self-confidence are able to spend more freely and enjoy life more fully because they "just know" that, come what may, they'll come out on top.

Herman has to learn to trust people, and mitzvahs are his ticket for reaching that goal. Trust is the key to forming and sustaining intimate relationships. Without close friends people become lonely and bored and often resort to extravagant diversions to fill their emptiness.

Blamers are another group who use the lack of money to smokescreen their joylessness.

"How can I be happy when my parents won't buy me a car, or give me the money to go on a ski trip or see Europe?" or "How can I enjoy myself when my husband/wife is a tightwad?"

Such statements are rubbish, and once clients develop self-confidence and/or trust, they stop blaming someone's stinginess for their unhappiness.

You would think down-and-outers—people who are barely getting by—would complain most about not enjoying themselves because of a lack of money.

Ironically, they usually complain the least. Perhaps it's because they've been forced by circumstances to find simple pleasures and are most apt to find amusement in such inexpensive activities as fishing, quilting bees, card playing, and gardening.

Let's talk a bit about the link between money and everyday joyfulness.

The passion for money and possessions usually masks an emotional hunger that cannot be satisfied by any degree of wealth or the accumulation of material goods. It is no coincidence that yuppies (acquisition-minded materialists) have surfaced at the very time that commitment-phobes (men and women who cannot sustain close long-term emotional relationships) have also become a lamentable phenomenon.

Is it tough to enjoy life when you're not sure where the bucks are coming from to pay the rent or put food on the table?

No question about it. Only in nineteen-thirties-style Hollywood fantasies do the financially strapped sing and dance their troubles away.

But there's more to be said about the money/joy connection. While there are many who, through no fault of their own, are barely getting by and deserve our compassion and help, most people today have economic safety nets—what with the ready availability of jobs, unemployment benefits, pension plans, medical care insurance, and social security—to be free of crushing poverty.

Many of those suffering serious financial distress have done it to themselves—by compulsive spending, overextension, loss of financial control—having bought into the myth that you need to spend lots of money to enjoy life more fully.

Sensible folk know that's not the case. History provides us with ample evidence that the rich and powerful often fall victim to their penchant for excess.

How about the wealthy? Aren't they happier?

Although no study has found that wealthy people are happier, a number of studies have found that the happiest people are more optimistic (they know they're winners), more trusting (they have close, loving relationships), more self-confident (they have the courage to confront challenges) more open-minded (they explore new ideas and activities), and more involved (are engaged in one or more absorbing activities).

Since money can't buy any one of the aforementioned characteristics, wealthy people are neither happier nor unhappier than others. Nor does increased income bring increased joy. The July/August 1989 issue of *Psychology Today* reports that surveys conducted between 1946 and 1978 (a period when real income rose dramatically) revealed Americans were no happier in the '70s than in the '40s.

Surprisingly, the majority of people past middle age are far too intent on accumulating wealth. Nationally prominent financial consultant Adriane Berg, author of *Your Wealth-Building Years,* finds that most people facing retirement "save more money than they'll ever get to spend. Less than two percent of all Americans die insolvent—with no liquid assets. The majority of golden-agers would be well advised to 'spend down'—pleasure themselves with the interest and dividends they're earning, instead of reinvesting them."

Is there a relationship between spending or saving and joy?

According to Dr. James R. Hodge, former chairman of the Department of Psychiatry at Northeastern Ohio University's College of Medicine: "Generally speaking, spending, saving, and joy are age-related. I've found that young people who *save* more enjoy life more—and old folks who *spend* more enjoy life more.

"More young people, especially singles," Hodge explains, "often wind up in hock because they spend more than they can afford and find it hard to enjoy life when faced with dunning letters and calls.

"On the other hand, many oldsters, particularly those conditioned to scrimp and save from years of struggling to raise a family, put kids through college, pay off a mortgage, and put a few bucks aside, find it difficult to spend freely even when they have the wherewithal to indulge themselves. There's no question but the overly frugal elderly would enjoy life more if they saved less."

Ms. Berg agrees: "Tough as it is to get young people to cut back, it's just as hard to get their elders to cut loose.

"When confronted by spendthrifts, I try to get them to recognize the basis for their overspending—that it's usually an attempt to buy love, impress others, or to escape boredom.

"When counseling penny-pinchers, I try to get them to realize their frugality is based on economic conditions that no longer exist. I give them the facts: Most who die are worth thousands, and I ask, 'Have you noticed not one of them has managed to take their money with them?'—and advise them to 'Go first class, or your heirs will!' "

SPENDING IS THE KEY

- If you keep getting into financial hot water, you'll enjoy life a lot more by spending a little less.
- If you habitually begrudge yourself affordable pleasures, you'll enjoy life a lot more by spending a little more.

It's not a question of saving—but of spending.

If you spend money to enhance the quality of your life and the lives of those around you and are not denying yourself attainable pleasures, you're on the right savings track.

Yes, you can enjoy yourself without making or spending big bucks—by delighting in many of life's inexpensive pleasures, like teaching a child to ride a bike, taking up a challenging craft, hobby, or sport, delving into an interesting subject, or simply watching birds flutter around a backyard bird feeder.

For example:

Gene Bon Vicini was fourteen when he arrived in this country from Italy and has struggled to earn a living in his adopted land his entire life. He has delivered groceries, mowed lawns, washed cars, sold papers, worked on construction sites, been a butcher and a day laborer.

Gene's a handyman and for years has spent his spare time creating wooden toys from scraps for his family's and friends' children. His only claim to fame: he's designed an untippable rocking horse, and over the past twenty years he's made and given away more than two hundred of these uniquely designed playthings to children's hospitals and nursery schools.

"There's nothing in the world to beat making a child happy," says Gene. "When I think of all the youngsters riding my rocking horses, it gladdens my heart and makes me smile."

That's not to deny that you can have fun *with* money. Here's a story about a well-heeled, admittedly eccentric lady who really knows how to get her kicks with big bucks.

The elegant dowager in question had driven her Mercedes to a crowded shopping center and was patiently waiting for the next car to vacate its parking place. But before she could maneuver her large-ish sedan into the empty slot, a young arrogant driver who had just appeared on the scene zipped his sports car into the spot rightfully hers. To add insult to injury the insolent intruder laughed at the lady's chagrin and called out, "That's what you can do when you're young and quick."

The matron hesitated, then rammed her luxury auto right into the rear end of the youth's car, smashing in the trunk. "That's what you can do when you're old and rich!" she sang out as she drove merrily away.

If you're still convinced that insufficient discretionary income is keeping you from enjoying life, maybe the next chapter will get you to change your mind, your spending habits, and your life.

To Enjoy Life More Fully You Must Keep Reminding Yourself That Life Is Too Short to Waste on Unhappiness

Not in Utopia—subterranean fields,—
Or some secreted island, Heaven knows where!
But in the very world, which is the world
Of all of us,—the place where, in the end
We find our happiness, or not at all!

> *The Prelude*
> William Wordsworth

9

Mortality Therapy: It Hurts, but It's Worth a Try!

It seems that at every turn we're being reminded to enjoy ourselves before it's too late. Friends and family remind us; bumper stickers, cards, T-shirts, and other paraphernalia broadcast the message; poets and songwriters advise us to make the most of our brief stay on planet earth.

> How far can you travel
> when you're six feet underground?*

> Gather ye rosebuds while ye may,
> Old Time is still a-flying:
> And this same flower that smiles to-day,
> To-morrow will be dying.**

> Time waits for no one.***

*"Enjoy Yourself"—Words, Herb Magidson; Music, Carl Sigman
**"To the Virgins, to Make Much of Time"—Robert Herrick
***"Time Waits for No One"—Words and Music by Cliff Friend and Charles Tobias

Lives of great men all remind us
  We can make our lives sublime,
And, departing, leave behind us
  Footprints on the sands of time.*

You can't take it with you!

There isn't a person we know who believes he or she is immortal—so why all the reminding?

It would appear that creative talents who take the time to inform us of something we already know are guilty of doing the very thing they advise us not to do—frittering away precious time. But are they onto something we may have overlooked? It's very likely.

Despite the fact that we *know* life is finite, don't many of us, deep down and to varying degrees, find the idea of death so abhorrent that we have difficulty accepting our mortality and, as a result, conveniently deny its reality?

How else could we explain such contradictory behavior as worrying about little things (and it's *all* little things) like accumulating money we'll never get to spend, delaying attainable pleasures, making ourselves miserable pleasing others, driving ourselves up a wall by living up to other people's expectations, burdening ourselves with impossible goals and self-destructive habits?

Is there a connection between our pleasure ability and our willingness to accept our mortality, or are we unable to enjoy life more fully because we're hampered by anxieties and fears?

It's not an either/or relationship. Socio-ability, changeability, and our concept of death all impact on our ability to enjoy ourselves.

*"A Psalm of Life"—Henry Wadsworth Longfellow

THE JOY-MORTALITY PARADOX

It would seem that people who repress gloomy thoughts of death would be freer to pursue life's pleasures, but actually the reverse is true.

Those who deny their mortality are inordinately anxious about death and find it tougher to enjoy themselves—while individuals who accept their mortality enjoy life more readily.

The point was brought home in the award-winning TV miniseries *Lonesome Dove.*

In one memorable scene, Laurie, a former prostitute, is sitting in the hot sun feeling sorry for herself because Jake, her gambler lover, who was taking her to San Francisco, has left her behind to do some card playing in Austin.

Gus, a former Texas Ranger, with a soft spot in his heart for Laurie, sees her moping outside her tent and rides over to comfort her. But nothing he offers to salve her sadness lifts her gloom, and so he says, "Well, what then? You name it."

And Laurie responds, "I just wanna go to San Francisco ... (tearfully) ... that's what I want."

To which Gus offers this uncommon wisdom: "Laurie, listen to me now, you pretty little thing. You see, life in San Francisco is still just life. Now, if you want only one thing too much, it's likely to turn out a disappointment. The only healthy way to live, as I see it, is to learn to like all the little everyday things ... like a sip of good whiskey of an evening, or a soft bed, or a glass of buttermilk, or a feisty gentleman like myself."

Gus, who had narrowly escaped death many times, had learned to live life day to day and to savor life's minor pleasures. Laurie, like others who have never faced the certainty of their mortality—or the likelihood of an unexpectedly early death—pushes such a possibility far out of mind and gambles that she has endless time to savor life's pleasures.

People can fool you, as well as themselves. Some who talk and behave as though they are fearlessly realistic about the inevitable end we all face are actually whistling in the dark, so to speak.

One fear-ridden lady, widowed and living alone, planned her funeral, paid for it in advance, arranged for eternal care for her burial spot, but gave herself away when she complained to her only daughter, who lived far away, "What will I do if I wake up some morning dead?"

If Laurie had recognized—or reported—her fear of death to the town doc, chances are he would have dismissed her complaint by telling her, "Everyone fears death. We're all in the same boat," or, "So what else is new?"

If she were to report her fear to a modern-day "shrink," he'd probably impart similar assurances. While mental health professionals are adept at helping people deal with other fears and phobias, when it comes to the fear of death they're not comfortable.

According to Dr. Leo Wollman, a noted psychiatrist, gerontologist, and endocrinologist, "Mental health practitioners are inept at helping patients and clients deal with the fear of death because they haven't been taught how—and if they were to be taught, many would be incapable of helping others because they're fearful of death themselves."

For years Dr. Wollman had been dissatisfied with the ineffectual assurances he gave death-fearing patients. Then, eleven years ago, a friend who was fearful of death told Wollman about a book he had read, *Life After Life,* by Dr. Raymond Moody. "It changed my life," declared the friend. "I'm not as scared of dying."

Over the past ten years Dr. Wollman has developed his unique Mortality Therapy, which has helped over three hundred patients reduce their fear of death.

MORTALITY THERAPY

The fear of death diminishes the capacity of people of all ages to enjoy themselves.

Though such fears escalate noticeably for many as they pass age fifty, they are not exclusive to older adults. There are large numbers of younger adults, even teenagers, who harbor an inordinate fear of dying.

If you cringe when you drive by a cemetery, avoid going to funerals, change the subject when death comes up in conversation, hate visiting someone in the hospital, you're probably overly fearful of death. If you're past fifty and haven't written a will, haven't seriously considered purchasing a cemetery plot, spend as little time as possible with aged or seriously ill people, you're probably unduly frightened of death.

Whatever your age, here's what you can do:

• **READ UP ON NEAR-DEATH EXPERIENCES.**

There are a number of books available that contain carefully documented testimonials from people who've nearly died. Survivors describe their near deaths in, for the most part, extremely positive terms. They report feelings of peace, painlessness, pleasantness, serenity, and suspension and tell of seeing, being enveloped by, or entering light and describe a remarkable sense of bodily separation. Such reports have primarily been made by those whose near death was caused by accident or illness. Attempted suicides rarely report such positive experiences.

Of the 520 patients and nonpatients Dr. Wollman has advised to read such books, 409 reported reduced death fears.

When asked whether their fear of death was altered by their reading, a typical response was, "Somewhat. I'm not nearly as fearful of dying—but even more wonderful, I feel as though a tremendous weight has been lifted off my chest."

Recommended reading: *Life after Life, The Light Beyond,* and *Reflections on Life after Life* by Dr. Raymond Moody; *Heading Toward Omega: In Search of the Meaning of the Near-Death Experience* and *Life at Death: A Scientific Investigation of the Near-Death Experience* by Kenneth Ring; *Living with Death and Dying* and *Working it Through* by Elisabeth Kübler-Ross.

• WRITE YOUR EULOGY AND WILL.

Bolster your newfound courage by facing up to your mortality.

In writing your eulogy pay particular attention to joy—the joy you've experienced and missed out on, the joy you've given and not given to family and friends.

In writing your will leave something to everyone who has touched your life—including your enemies.

One elderly gentleman who was particularly fearful of death balked when Dr. Wollman suggested he write his will. He was superstitious and was convinced that once he designated heirs to his estate, he would surely die; nevertheless, he did agree.

When Wollman met him two weeks later he was ecstatic.

"What happened?" he asked.

"That will idea is what happened. I can't remember ever feeling so great. I wrote the will like you said and left my no-good lazy son-in-law a year's supply of Ex-Lax to get his ass moving!"

"If you're into getting even," said Wollman, "your best revenge is living well."

When writing your will, consider donating your organs. The following letter, written by Robert Test and published in Abigail

Van Buren's "Dear Abby" column, may help you make a determination:

To Remember Me

At a certain moment a doctor will determine that my brain has ceased to function and that, for all intents and purposes, my life has stopped.

When that happens, do not attempt to instill artificial life into my body by the use of a machine. And don't call this my "deathbed." Call it my "bed of life," and let my body be taken from it to help others lead fuller lives.

Give my sight to a man who has never seen a sunrise, a baby's face, or love in the eyes of a woman.

Give my heart to a person whose own heart has caused nothing but endless days of pain.

Give my blood to the teenager who has been pulled from the wreckage of his car, so that he can live to see his grandchildren play.

Give my kidneys to one who depends on a machine to exist from week to week.

Take my bones, every muscle, every fiber and nerve in my body, and find a way to make a crippled child walk.

Explore every corner of my brain. Take my cells if necessary and let them grow so that someday a speechless boy will shout at the crack of a bat and a deaf girl will hear the sound of rain against her windows.

Burn what is left of me and scatter the ashes to the winds to help the flowers grow.

If you must bury something, let it be my faults, my weaknesses, and all prejudice against my fellowman.

Give my soul to God.

If by chance you wish to remember me, do it with a kind deed or word to someone who needs you. If you do all I have asked, I will live forever. —Robert N. Test

(For donor forms, write to The Living Bank, P.O. Box 6725, Houston, Texas 77265.)

• PRETEND YOU HAVE ONLY A SHORT TIME LEFT TO LIVE.

When people with a terminal illness find out they have only a short time to live, they invariably look back on their lives wishing they had spent more time enjoying themselves—fewer hours working and more attending Little League games, spending time with their spouse, pleasuring themselves.

Many start living differently—they devote more time to their families, become more sensitive to the beauty around them, are more touching and loving, more open and trusting, don't push as hard to make money or achieve success, take a long-delayed trip, and make every effort to enjoy what days remain.

We are all afflicted with a fatal illness called life. The only difference between most of us and those who have been given the bad news is we are less sure as to how much time we have left.

Why wait until a medical diagnosis shocks you into adding more life to your days? Why wait until you face death before you start learning how to live?

After Gilda Radner died of ovarian cancer, her husband, Gene Wilder, said it best: "Life is very short. You never know that. You hear it, you know to say it. But when you see illness around, that's when you know it's true. Everyone says, 'I know, I know,' but they don't know s—— from Shinola. If they knew, they'd stop doing what's unimportant and do what's important. There's no time for anything else. And it's too sad to learn it when it's too late."

If still unconvinced, pretend this is your last day on earth. How will you spend it? Chances are you'll chuck your diet and eat dessert first!

• PINCH YOURSELF INTO LIVING WELL.

Should you get up on the wrong side of the bed, before you give up on the day pinch a sensitive spot on your body to remind yourself that life is too short to waste even one day.

Should you meet up with discouragements, setbacks, rudeness, or delays, before you start aggravating yourself pinch a sensitive spot to remind yourself that life is too precious to waste on aggravation.

Should you agree to a request you regret having agreed to, before you make yourself miserable pinch a sensitive spot to remind yourself that you can't waste your life making everybody happy but yourself.

Should you start thinking about things that may go wrong, before you start agonizing pinch a sensitive spot to remind yourself to stop worrying your life away.

Should you regret not having done something, before you start feeling guilty pinch a sensitive spot to remind yourself to get cracking. More people regret what they didn't do than what they did do.

Should you regret having hurt someone, before you add guilt to your regret pinch a sensitive spot to remind yourself that life is too short to waste on guilt—then ask for forgiveness.

• PUT YOURSELF TO THE TOMBSTONE TEST.

Ask yourself, "If I died tomorrow, how would I want my tombstone to read? That I made a mound of money? That I gave my all to becoming successful? That I enjoyed life to the fullest?"

If you want to be remembered as a loving person, somewhat successful, who never lost sight of the importance of bringing happiness to yourself and others, it's not too soon to start restructuring your life to that end.

Read the obituary columns occasionally, and you'll be alerted to how trivial someone's press-worthy achievements seem after death.

One example that comes readily to mind: When the "pioneer of Tex-Mex cuisine" died, the obituary column noted his two main achievements in life—having created a crisp taco shell and smothering his enchiladas in sour cream.

In 1983 forty-two-year-old Senator Paul Tsongas learned he had lymphoma (an incurable yet treatable form of cancer). The diagnosis triggered some serious thoughts about the meaning of life. First, he quit the political rat race to devote more time to his family. Then he wrote about it, in his book *Heading Home:*

> The illness made me face up to the fact that I will die someday. It made me think about wanting to look back without regret whenever that happened. It made me appreciate [his wife] Niki's strengths as I had never quite done before. I am blessed with a marriage that provides meaning. I would now look at my wife and "see" her in a way that one does not do in the rush of everyday life.

The lymphoma caused me to realize the preciousness of the moments of a child's development. I would have spent too much time away from my daughters had I continued my career. The adventure and the power would have been seductive. . . .

But I would not have helped Ashley on her science project or accompanied Katina on her Brownie weekend camping trip or had Molly fall asleep in my arms on the hammock. [Ashley, Katina, and Molly were, at the time, Senator Tsongas's nine-, six-, and two-year-old daughters.]

Life is a search for balance. We all have to bring the scales back to center.

Finally, my illness has forced me to understand that I have true spiritual needs whether I am healthy or unhealthy. It's hard to write about this. But I find I must attend church services in order to renew and refresh my sense of a higher being. . . .

These changes . . . are a precious gift. The cancer gave them to me. I treasure them, and I will curse myself if I ever begin to forget, if I ever take my present health for granted, if I ever let a day pass when I don't feel gratitude that it has been given to me.

I notice if the sky is blue now. I see that God has given us the flowers and the rivers and the sunshine. I realize that life is wondrous in its natural and human dimensions.

Senator Tsongas credits his cancer for his precious gifts—and rightly so.

Now forty-eight, he has had six years to live life without regrets. Many who are advanced in age, who suffer a heart attack or discover they have cancer or some other debilitating disease, have little time left to reorder their priorities.

We are all merely mortal. The trick is to live as though you believe it—to enjoy life before death.

TO LIFE!

You Can Turn Your Life Around By Changing What You Say and Do

When someone says, "I can't change," some part of them wants to change, but the payoffs for his present behavior are greater than the payoffs for a changed behavior, or his fear of change is too great.

—Dr. Harold Greenwald
psychologist and author of
Direct Decision Therapy

10

Pinches and Pats

Our behavior and attitudes are shaped and fashioned, influenced and modified, by the consequences of what we do and say. We've already suggested self-inflicted punishments (pinches) for joy-killing behavior. How about some self-administered rewards (pats) to reinforce joyful behavior?

HOW TO KEEP REMINDING YOURSELF TO ENJOY LIFE

• Remind yourself to take the time to enjoy life by eating dessert first.

Occasionally start your meal with dessert. Savor the treat and tell yourself, "I'm eating dessert first to remind myself to take the time to enjoy the many sweet things life has to offer."

• Remind yourself to enjoy the fruits of your labor by going first class.

Once in a while treat yourself to designer-label clothing, first-class airline tickets, front-row theater seats, dinner in a four-star restaurant, a top-of-the-line appliance, and tell yourself, "I'm going first class to remind myself I deserve the best."

• Remind yourself to enjoy the things you have by making frequent use of your fine possessions.

Kick your "Sunday best" habit. Make use of any finery you've stored away for a special occasion—fine linens, dinnerware, silverware, jewelry. Don't wait for company to eat in the dining room, put candles on the table, decorate with fresh flowers, cook special meals. When you buy something new, wear it or use it right away and when you do, tell yourself, "I'm enjoying the fine things I own to remind myself that it's foolish to put off attainable pleasures."

• Remind yourself that you are competent by celebrating past successes.

When concerned about the future, spend some time taking pride in your achievements—both spiritual and material—and tell yourself, "My accomplishments assure me that I can make dreams come true."

• Remind yourself that you don't need a lot of money to enjoy life.

From time to time see how much pleasure you can experience without spending a dime. Visit a bakery and smell freshly baked bread, study a bird in flight, admire a sunset, walk through autumn leaves, build a snowman or sand castle, daydream and fantasize, and as you do, tell yourself, "It's great to be alive." Take advantage of free concerts, block parties, museum exhibits, art shows, open-to-the-public lectures, sidewalk entertainers, and street fairs.

• Remind yourself of your good fortune by spending more time with loved ones.

Play games with your kids, take them to the zoo or circus, redecorate your little girl's dollhouse, go dancing, fishing, boating, bowling, window shopping, jogging, make love with your spouse, throw a lucky-me party for your family or friends, and tell yourself, "I'm truly fortunate to be surrounded by people I can love and who love me."

• Take on the role of family "fun-ancial" adviser.

Assume the responsibility of discovering fun things to do on a regular basis. Read the movie reviews to select the most promising new flicks; follow the food critics' recommendations on the best dining spots; study the what's-happening-this-weekend section of your daily paper to unearth amusing area events; stay on the lookout for entertaining community activities; keep in touch with friends and relatives to plan regular get-togethers. Find reasons to make merry: celebrate the first homegrown tomato ripe enough to eat, a kind word from the boss, a safe return from a long plane or auto trip, the Chinese New Year.

Why wait for birthdays to celebrate? "Mirth-days"—those times when you feel good for no particular reason—are a convenient excuse for partying whenever the urge hits. Develop the "mirth-day" habit, and you'll build a backlog of happy memories that will see you through less festive times.

• Set up a "happy" checklist.

The surest way to enjoy more personal happiness is to increase the frequency of positive, wonderful experiences in your life. That's something many of us forget to do.

Make an inventory of the things that please you, that give you a sparkle, that you don't indulge in often enough. Taking a long walk in the country with your spouse may be something you enjoy, but perhaps it's been six months since you've done that. A checklist will remind you to set aside time for all those things that give you real pleasure.

REPLACE DOWNER RESPONSES

Words can modify self-defeating attitudes and behavior.

Stay alert for opportunities to turn automatic, ordinary downbeat expressions into upbeat responses.

• When asked how you feel, instead of responding, "Fine," or "About the same," or "I can't complain," regardless of how you actually feel, try "Great," or "Fantastic," or "Wonderful," and you'll be surprised at how much better things will seem.

• Instead of using the expression "The problem is ..." try "A possible solution is ..." and you'll be pleased at how much better you'll feel focusing on solutions rather than getting bogged down in vexing situations.

• Instead of saying, "If the worse comes to the worst ..." try "If the worst comes to the best ..." or "One way or another I'll work things out," and you'll be uplifted by your newfound optimism.

• Instead of asking yourself, "How could I be so dumb?" try "Now and then I'm entitled to make a mistake." You'll be a much happier person giving yourself (and others) permission to be wrong on occasion.

• Instead of asking yourself, "Why me?" try "You win some, you lose some," and you'll be surprised at how much more you'll enjoy life when you learn to roll with the punches.

• Instead of telling yourself, "No one really understands me," try "I'll be better understood when I communicate my thoughts and feelings."

• Instead of "I should," "I must," "I'll try," or "If only," try "I'll do my best," "I will," or, "I can."

What's more—wipe that frown off your face. University researchers have confirmed what we've long suspected—an unpleasant look on your face (sadness, disgust, anger, anxiety) will trigger equally unpleasant physiological changes.

ANY QUESTIONS?

The expression "Eat dessert first" triggers many responses and questions. Here are some of the more common:

• *"It sounds frivolous and Pollyanna-ish. There's more to life than fun and games!"*

Agreed—but we followed the advice of Samuel Johnson, who wrote, "A book should teach us to enjoy life, or to endure it."

There are plenty of grim books around addressing the problems posed by serious physical and psychological disorders. This book was written to be helpful to the vast majority of normal neurotics—people like you and me, healthy enough to know we've got it good, but wise enough to realize that with a little enlightened effort, life could be better.

• *"Aren't desserts fattening?"*

Not if you eat desserts first. (See Chapter Twelve for more about desserts and weight control.)

• *"Do workaholics enjoy life?"*

No—they enjoy work. Life is made up of many things—play, rest, love, companionship, et cetera, and those whose sole pleasure is work are more vulnerable to depression when they suffer a career setback.

• *"Aren't people who are out to enjoy themselves selfish and irresponsible?"*

Not if they also find joy in making life more enjoyable for others. There's no reason to assume the pursuit of enjoyment goes hand in hand with selfishness and irresponsibility. Quite the reverse is often the case.

Haven't you noticed that people who don't put a high priority on pleasure are a pain? Let's not get sidetracked by the extremists. Truly joyous people who know how to pleasure themselves without taking advantage of others are a delight to have around. Indeed, they are generally more willing than most to occasionally sacrifice to make someone else happy. For example: They'll attend a function, gathering, or party they don't want to go to, to please someone they love—and they'll do so without rancor or resentment.

• *"What do you do when you give and give and someone takes advantage of you?"*

You stop giving to that person. Only give what and when you want to and only to whom you please.

Some people can be trusted, some cannot. It's not to your advantage to keep trusting someone who abuses your trust.

• *"Will people notice a change if I follow the advice in this book?"*

Don't count on people telling you how much nicer you seem. On the other hand, you can expect people to stop asking such questions as "Is there something bothering you?" or "Are you angry about something?"

• *"How come you failed to mention a sense of humor?"*

Sorry. A sense of humor doesn't make people joyous. Joyousness makes for a sense of humor.

You can't teach people to have a sense of humor. When people lower their social and change anxiety they stop taking themselves as seriously and, as a consequence, begin laughing at themselves—and that's how one develops a sense of humor.

• *"Is there a relationship between joy and health?"*

Most medical people believe so.

A joyless attitude toward the world—as evidenced by a basic disbelief in the goodness of your fellowman—is bad for your health, researchers confirm. Employees who don't trust their bosses, store clerks who have contempt for customers, businessmen out to get theirs any way they can, and ordinary people who have contempt for other ordinary people have a four- to five-times higher incidence of coronary heart disease.

Hard to believe?

In one study of 118 lawyers whose personalities were evaluated on a standard psychological test in 1963, twenty percent of those who were judged as having the highest hostility rating were dead by age fifty. Of those with the lowest I-hate-my-fellowman scores, only four percent had died after twenty-five years. No other health risk factor—not smoking, alcohol use, diet, exercise, et cetera, was found to be as positively related to the group's mortality rates as the degree of cynical mistrust of others.

According to Dr. Robert Ornstein, who, with Dr. David Sobel, authored *Healthy Pleasures,* "For most, living a happy life is much more important to our health than all the regimens we could undertake."

Their study finds that people who are especially healthy and robust tend to ignore standard advice about diet and exercise, and shared a common sense of optimism and an orientation toward pleasure.

"Improving your health doesn't necessarily mean giving up things you love, doing arduous exercises, or constantly worrying about everything you do," says Dr. Sobel. "It's often just following the things that give you pleasure … listening to music, smelling sweet scents, even going shopping may have unrecognized health benefits.

"Pleasure is a vital nutrient, and many people today are not getting their minimum daily requirement."

Evidently lightening a heavy heart is more important to your health than diet and exercise.

RULE ELEVEN

*Keep the Faith.
"When the Mind Is Ready,
a Teacher Appears."*
—*ZEN EXPRESSION*

11

Are You Ready to Enjoy Life More Fully?
... or are you stuck on hold?

Wishing and wanting to get more out of life won't cut it if, for whatever reason, you're unwilling to take a chance.

> Dear Dr. Gordon,
>   I'm divorced, raising two children on my own, and I'm a telephone operator trapped in a dead end job. I'd like to remarry and have a better life, but the few men I meet are just out for a good time.
>   I read your book *When Living Hurts* [a book to help people deal with emotional pain] and it hasn't helped. Is there something I'm doing wrong?

The above letter is typical of those Sol receives from readers who claim they've followed his suggestions and are still not happy.

Nobody has all the answers, but when someone is not making

progress, it's usually because the payoffs (advantages) of *not* changing outweigh the payoffs of changing.

Change is often chancy—there are no guarantees—and before anyone can fully commit to anxiety-provoking attitude and behavior changes, they must first convince themselves the rewards will be worth the risk—and that's not always obvious.

Good advice often falls on deaf ears simply because the listener is not ready to give up the payoffs for *not* changing.

The leading payoffs for complainers are sympathy and reassurance. Emotionally dependent individuals find it difficult to give up the compassion and comforting they elicit when they gripe, grouse, and growl, play the victim, and blame their misfortunes on circumstances beyond their control.

Complaining can also pay off as an ego booster. When you find fault with a product, service, or situation that others find satisfactory, doesn't that prove you are more quality conscious, have better taste and higher standards than others? Persons with low self-esteem have a difficult time relinquishing the temporary superiority they experience from downgrading other people's life-styles.

And the blamer? He gets to shed responsibility for anything that's gone wrong. Individuals who feel incompetent or incapable of bettering their lot in life shift focus from the part they've played by claiming, "Not my fault I'm so unhappy. It's because I was born poor, or ugly, or slow at learning, or have rotten parents." Thus "blamers" free themselves from having to improve their circumstances.

Here are some ways people lock themselves into unhappiness:

Bess L. is married to a car salesman who is a gambler and a

womanizer. She stays married, she claims, because she married "for better or worse." The truth: She's fearful of the loneliness and economic hardship she'd be likely to face as a divorcée.

Ron H., a supermarket employee, has turned down two promotions. His excuse: He doesn't want to sacrifice "family time" for the extra work time career advancement might entail. The truth: He's fearful he couldn't live up to the additional responsibility.

Rose S., a thirty-four-year-old well-to-do married woman with a teenage daughter, has for fifteen years complained to her husband that her parenting and household responsibilities have kept her from fulfilling her lifelong ambition—to be an attorney. The real reason she hasn't gone back to college is because she's afraid she wouldn't make the grade.

Hubert O., a psychologist, has been divorced for six years. Since his divorce he's been seriously interested in several women, but in each case decided against marriage. His explanation is "Marriage doesn't work anymore." The real reason he remains single is that he distrusts women.

Elaine F. is a thirty-four-year-old teacher who lives with her parents. Though envious of friends who have their own apartments, she's continued to stay with her parents. Why? She's afraid that on her own she'd be lonely and unable to afford the luxuries she currently enjoys.

Arthur B. is a struggling advertising copywriter, who is convinced that his doting mother is responsible for his mediocre achievements. He turns down career opportunities—not because he's incompetent, but because he's hell-bent on proving that his mother programmed him for failure.

Susan G., a twenty-six-year-old airline stewardess, complains that she's bored, tired, and lonely. When opportunities arise for meeting someone new, she invariably refuses, claiming she's too busy, when the truth is that she's leery of intimate relationships.

Sidney R.'s lifelong ambition has been to learn to play the piano. As a young man he felt he couldn't spare the time. As a husband and father he felt family responsibilities were too pressing. Now that he's divorced and retired, he still talks about "playing the piano someday" but can't get around to it. The one thing Sidney has learned is how to play it safe—to protect himself from chancing the discomfort of a new challenge. Maybe someday he'll learn to play a harp.

None of the above individuals was ready for change. It's as if they'd fed the pros and cons into their mental computers and came up with a thumbs-down on change. They can be compared to extremely cautious investors who are looking for maximum yield at minimum risk. They want a greater return on their investment and are unwilling to take the chance.

If you're in a holding pattern—or unable to see your way out of a blind alley—don't give up hope. There's a good chance that sometime in the not too distant future, before life becomes too painful, you'll be ready to do what's necessary to break free.

*   *   *

Monique G., a student of Sol's, found life had become unbearable because she was friendless.

Born and raised in Alabama, she moved to Syracuse to live with her aunt after her parents' divorce and, since her arrival, had felt like an outsider.

Her aunt, worried because her niece had become increasingly withdrawn, called and expressed her concern. Sol offered his help.

"Monique is a good girl," she said, "but because she's from the rural South, she feels like nobody wants to have anything to do with her."

At the urging of her aunt, Monique came to Sol after school and tearfully poured her heart out. "I was brought up to know my place," she said, "because people don't like it when you get too friendly."

They talked at length, and Sol counseled her daily. He told her to expect the best, not the worst, from people; to get the chip off her shoulder, to give her classmates a chance to befriend her; to expect to be treated as an equal.

To reinforce the advice and make it stick he told her to spend ten to twenty minutes a day picturing herself the most popular girl in school—to "see" herself being welcomed and accepted by schoolmates, invited to parties, and being a more trusting person.

About three months later Monique had been invited to join a sorority, was a member of the cheerleading squad, had been voted class secretary, and was part of the "in" crowd.

After her final session she brought Sol a gift, hugged him good-bye, and thanked him.

"You know, Dr. Gordon," she said, "what you told me was

right—and it worked. But my aunt told me the same things you told me."

"So why did you need me?" Sol asked.

She shrugged her shoulders and said, "I dunno."

"Because you weren't ready to listen," Sol said with a smile. "There's an old Zen expression that goes, When the mind is ready, a teacher appears."

RULE TWELVE

Life Is Uncertain . . .
Eat Dessert First!

12

Reaping Your Just Desserts

The phrase EAT DESSERT FIRST is meaningful on two levels.

Philosophically, it suggests enjoyment should be your top priority—that you should reassess your priorities and stop putting joy on the back burner.

Taken literally, it implies there's an advantage to eating dessert when you feel like it, that doing so blunts early training that programmed you to expect dessert—or pleasure—only after you've earned it or paid the price.

Children are told, "No dessert until you've eaten all your vegetables"; "You can't go out and play until you've finished your homework"; "If you behave yourself at the dentist's, he'll give you a lollipop"; "I'll give you your allowance after you walk the dog, clean your room, take out the garbage, mow the lawn."

Powerful conditioning ... and it sticks!

The corporate world has capitalized on such training. Some land-sales companies, for example, entice would-be investors with a gourmet meal in a luxury hotel, then—to make certain their prospects sit through the sales pitch—withhold dessert until the presentation is over.

Brought up to think of desserts—and pleasures—as somewhat sinful, many of us equate enjoyment with the illegal, immoral—or worse yet, fattening!

Not so! Taken as a metaphor for living, the admonition to EAT DESSERT FIRST! is a gentle reminder to pleasure yourself whenever you can.

Taken literally, EAT DESSERT FIRST! means just what the words say—and the good news is, it's good for you, even if you're overweight or want to keep your weight down.

The astute health expert who first noted and documented the astonishing benefits of eating dessert first is Dr. Maria Simonson, professor emeritus at Johns Hopkins Medical Institutions and director of the Health, Weight, and Stress Clinic. Here's what she says:

"Many adults are overweight because they were force-fed by mothers who used dessert as an end-of-the-meal reward. The no-dessert-until-you've-finished-dinner ploy encourages eating more food than you wish to reach a desirable goal. As a result you're stuffed by the time you get dessert—gorged afterward."

Dr. Simonson's controlled studies of hundreds of overweight subjects have revealed that dieters who eat a low-calorie dessert *before* their meal eat less and lose more weight than those who have dessert last or no dessert at all.

"It's a matter of blood-sugar levels," explains Simonson. "When they're elevated, your appetite diminishes."

Eliminating desserts while dieting is a big mistake, she warns.

"Deprived dieters tend to binge and go off their diets more readily than dieters who have a little dessert prior to eating."

How much is a little?

"Enough to satisfy the taste buds is all right. More than that is too much! Leave room for a nutritionally balanced meal.

"When eating out share your dessert. If you find no takers, have it wrapped up and take it home as a delightful appetite suppressor for a number of meals."

OTHER DESSERT MYTHS

• MYTH: Desserts are "empty calorie" foods with no re-deeming nutritional value.

• FACT: Most desserts, especially those containing chocolate, egg, milk, cheese, and fruits, contain ample amounts of protein, calcium, iron, Vitamin A, thiamin, and riboflavin.

• MYTH: Desserts are bad for your teeth.

• FACT: Not when you eat dessert at the start of a meal. The increased saliva flow combats oral bacteria. Eating desserts between meals is not recommended—but if you must, brush your teeth after snacks. Worst of all is the nosh at bedtime, when saliva production is almost at a standstill.

If you still find it hard to believe you can enjoy desserts without wrecking your diet, here are some of our favorite recipes for guiltless gorging for the thin-at-heart. They're ways weight watchers can once again have their cake and eat it too—light but luscious treats for the virtuous from Arline Brecher's kitchen. We will continue with Judith Gordon's rec-ommendations for the occasional treats for the not-so-virtuous lovers of desserts.

But before we splurge, let us review our twelve steps for a more joyful life.

When Living Hurts, Joy Relieves the Pain

To Be More Joyful You Must Accept Responsibility for Your Happiness

The Less You Justify Joylessness the More You'll Enjoy Life

You Can Talk Yourself into and out of Joylessness

To Maximize Joy You Must Minimize Anxiety

Help Yourself to Happiness by Bringing Joy to Others

To Conquer Fear You Must Feign Courage

It's Not How Well Money Is Saved, But How Well It's Spent, that Determines Joyfulness

To Enjoy Life More Fully You Must Keep Reminding Yourself that Life Is Too Short to Waste on Unhappiness

You Can Turn Your Life Around by Changing What You Say and Do

Keep the Faith. "When the Mind Is Ready, a Teacher Appears."

Life Is Uncertain ... Eat Dessert First!

Fruitful Lifeboats

16-ounce carton of vanilla-flavored low-fat yogurt
1 ripe pineapple
1 pint fresh strawberries, hulled and chopped
2 tbsps. brown sugar

Drain yogurt.

Cut pineapple into quarters lengthwise. Remove flesh, keeping shell in one piece, including leaves. Chop fruit.

Mix strawberries with sugar and set aside.

Place yogurt in a medium-sized bowl. Add pineapple and strawberries, stirring gently with a fork until well blended.

Spoon into pineapple shells, chill, and serve to 4 lucky people.

Kvellabration Cherry Chocolate Brownie Bars

16-ounce carton vanilla-flavored yogurt
¾ cup water
2 tbsps. unflavored gelatin
5 tbsps. unsweetened cocoa
½ cup black cherry fruit spread
3 egg whites
¼ cup sugar

Drain yogurt.
Preheat oven to 325 degrees.
Soften gelatin in ¼ cup of water for 5 minutes.
Heat ½ cup water and stir in cocoa and gelatin. Stir until dissolved. Cool slightly.
Place yogurt in a medium-sized bowl. Add cherry spread, stirring gently with a fork or wire whisk until well blended. Gradually blend in gelatin mixture.
In a separate bowl, beat egg whites until foamy. Gradually add sugar and continue to beat until moist, soft peaks form when beater is withdrawn. Fold into yogurt mixture.
Pour into an 8-inch-square pie pan and bake 30 minutes.
Cool on a wire rack. Refrigerate until chilled. Cut into squares to serve eight eager celebrants.

Apricot Raspberry Compote with Chutzpah

½ cup sugar
1 tbsp. bourbon
6 to 7 apricots
1 cup raspberries
⅛ tsp. nutmeg
½ cup vanilla yogurt

Combine the sugar and ½ cup water in a microwavable bowl.

Microwave on high until sugar is dissolved and the mixture is hot—about 4 minutes.

Stir in the bourbon and let cool.

Halve and pit the apricots. Gently toss the apricots, raspberries, and cooled syrup together.

Stir the nutmeg into the yogurt.

Serve the fruit topped with the yogurt to 4 of your favorite people.

Better Days Buttermilk Lemon Sherbet

1 quart buttermilk
1 tbsp. grated lemon peel
¼ cup lemon juice
⅓ cup sugar
1½ cups light corn syrup

Pour buttermilk into large mixing bowl. Add remaining ingredients and stir until well blended.

Pour into freezing tray or loaf pan and freeze quickly until mixture is a mush (about 1 hour).

Meantime, chill the mixing bowl. Turn mixture into chilled bowl and beat with rotary beater until smooth.

Return to tray and freeze until firm. (About 3 hours.) Enough to serve 8 fun-loving dinner guests.

A Light but Luscious Trifle

2 packages vanilla pudding-and-pie-filling mix
1 quart milk
2 tbsps. sugar
1 tbsp. vanilla
1 package (3 oz.) ladyfingers
⅓ cup strawberry preserves
½ cup macaroon or vanilla wafer crumbs

In a medium saucepan, combine pudding mix, milk, and sugar, mixing well.

Cook over medium heat, stirring constantly, until mixture thickens and comes to a boil. Stir in vanilla.

Split ladyfingers. Fill with preserves and put together again.

In a 2-quart serving dish, place a layer of one fourth of the ladyfingers, cookie crumbs, and pudding. Repeat three times, ending with pudding.

Refrigerate three hours. Garnish with additional dots of strawberry preserves and serve to 10 fortunate dessert lovers.

Almost Like Mama's Old-World Apple-Noodle Pudding

---

    6 oz. wide egg noodles
    1 tbsp. salt
    3 to 4 quarts boiling water
    ¼ cup unsalted, polyunsaturated margarine, softened
    ¼ cup granulated sugar
    ¼ cup orange juice
    1 can (21 oz.) apple pie filling
    1 medium apple, sliced
    ¼ cup golden raisins
    ¾ cup cornflakes, crushed
    ¼ cup firmly packed light-brown sugar

Gradually add noodles and salt to rapidly boiling water so that water continues to boil. Cook, uncovered, stirring occasionally until tender.

Drain in colander. Add margarine to hot noodles and toss until melted.

Add all remaining ingredients except cornflakes and brown sugar; toss gently until combined. Turn into shallow 1½-quart casserole.

Mix crushed cornflakes with brown sugar and sprinkle over surface of pudding.

Bake uncovered at 350 degrees for 35 to 40 minutes, or until apples are tender. Serve warm to 6 people who have fond memories of Mama's desserts.

Lick the Blues Blueberry Mousse

1 cup port wine
1 tbsp. grated orange rind
½ tsp. ground cinnamon
1 pint (2 cups) fresh or frozen blueberries
¼ cup cold water
1 tbsp. unflavored gelatin
3 egg whites, at room temperature
½ cup sugar

Heat port wine in a medium-size saucepan over moderate heat until it boils. Turn off heat, then blaze by igniting. Let flame die, then return to heat.

Add orange rind and cinnamon. Cover and simmer gently for 10 minutes.

Add blueberries and cook for 1 minute. Pour into a bowl and cool to room temperature.

Place the water in a small saucepan and sprinkle with gelatin. Allow to stand 10 minutes, then dissolve over low heat.

Stir gelatin into the blueberry mixture, place over a bowl of ice, and stir until mixture thickens.

Beat the egg whites until glossy, gradually adding sugar until stiff peaks form. Stir one third of the beaten whites into the blueberry mixture.

Fold in remaining whites and pour carefully into a serving dish.

Place in freezer until firm. Remove from freezer and store in refrigerator 20 to 30 minutes before serving to 7 or 8 upbeat people.

That's not to suggest you should never go all out. Every once in a while indulge in a dessert that's truly decadent.

Malcolm Forbes, the multimillionaire business-magazine publisher, balloonist, motorcyclist, wine connoisseur, and dessert lover, who has established a well-deserved reputation for living life to the fullest, was recently spied rounding out a gourmet meal with chocolate mousse cake—whereupon he said, "Dessert has always been my favorite vegetable. To me, having just fruit for dessert reminds me of being a little kid and getting clothes for Christmas. What kind of treat is that?"

When you're in the mood to go whole hog and indulge in some sinful concoctions, try one of these wicked recipes recommended by Judith Gordon:

Trifle—the Real Thing

1 heaping tbsp. flour
4 cups milk
2 eggs
3 tbsp. sugar
6 tbsp. cream sherry
Cake: angel food, pound, or any stale white cake
1½ lbs. strawberry jam
1 pint heavy cream
Maraschino cherries for decoration

Mix the flour with a little of the milk.

Heat remaining milk just to the boiling point, and pour over the flour mixture, mixing thoroughly.

Beat the eggs and sugar well and add to the flour and milk.

Pour back into the pan and bring to a boil, stirring constantly.

Break stale cake into pieces and spread liberally with strawberry jam. Layer all of this into a serving bowl and soak with sherry. Pour the custard mixture carefully over the entire concoction, and store in refrigerator overnight. Before serving, whip the cream and "dollop" it over the custard mixture and decorate with maraschino cherries.

When serving, wait for applause and refrain from telling anyone how hard you worked.

Live It Up Lebkuchen

---

2 cups sugar
4 sticks butter
12 eggs
½ cup dark molasses
4 cups flour
1 tsp. nutmeg
1 tsp. cinnamon
1 tsp. allspice
½ tsp. cloves
1½ lbs. crystallized fruit (mixed)
1 lb. golden raisins
3 cups chopped pecans
½ cup bourbon
½ cup cocoa

Chop all fruits, nuts, and raisins. Sprinkle with ¼ cup flour.

Cream butter and sugar, adding eggs one at a time. Add molasses and spices. Sift all dry ingredients together and add.

Next, add fruits, nuts, raisins, then bourbon.

Pour into well-greased pans about 1½ inches thick and bake in 350-degree oven about 45 minutes. When cold, ice with plain white icing, cut into squares, and serve to people who appreciate the good life.

Heavenly Hash Delight

1 stick butter
1 cup sugar
4 eggs
1 large can (16 oz.) Hershey's chocolate syrup
1 cup flour
1 tsp. baking powder
1 small package miniature marshmallows

Blend together butter, sugar, and eggs. Mix well.
Add flour and baking powder.
Bake in greased and floured 13″ × 9″ pan for thirty minutes at 350 degrees. Remove from oven and cover first with marshmallows, then with the following topping:

1 stick butter
2 tbsp. cocoa
1 egg
2 cups 10X sugar
1 tbsp. vanilla
1 cup chopped nuts

Melt butter with cocoa over direct low heat. Remove from stove and beat in egg, powdered sugar, vanilla, and nuts. Spread over cake.

Cheer-Up Cheesecake

2 pkgs. (8-oz. size) cream cheese
1 lb. creamed cottage cheese
1½ cups sugar
4 eggs, slightly beaten
3 tbsp. cornstarch
3 tbsp. flour
2 tsp. lemon juice
½ cup butter, melted
1 package graham cracker crumbs
1 pint sour cream

Preheat oven to 325 degrees. Press graham cracker crumbs in buttered springform.

In larger mixer bowl, beat cream cheese and cottage cheese until creamy. Gradually beat in sugar and eggs. Add remaining ingredients. Bake 1 hour and 10 minutes.

Richly Deserved Rice Dessert

2 cups cooked rice
1 pint heavy cream
1 tsp. vanilla extract
1 small package slivered almonds
1 can bing cherries in heavy syrup

Cook rice in milk. Let it cool completely. Whip cream and fold it into rice. Add vanilla and slivered almonds. Refrigerate.

Just before serving, heat cherries in a saucepan. Dish out rice dessert, along with hot cherries in a sauceboat.

Chocolate Decadence

---

1 lb. semisweet chocolate, broken into squares
10 tbsp. (1¼ sticks) sweet butter
4 eggs
1 tbsp. sugar
1 tbsp. flour

TOPPING:
1½ cups heavy cream
1 tbsp. vanilla extract
1 tbsp. sugar
Shaved chocolate
1 pkg. (10 or 12 ounces) frozen raspberries, defrosted

Butter and flour an 8-inch cake pan and line it with paper.
Preheat oven to 425 degrees.

Cake: Put the chocolate and butter in the top of a double
boiler and heat until the chocolate is just melted. Set aside.

In the top of another double boiler beat the eggs and sugar
until the sugar dissolves and the mixture thickens and is about
quadrupled in volume.

Fold the flour into the thickened egg mixture. Stir a quarter
of the flour-egg mixture into the melted chocolate, then fold
the chocolate into the remaining egg mixture. Pour the batter
into the prepared cake pan. Shake it gently to level it. Bake for
15 minutes. The cake will still be gooey and seemingly un-
cooked. Cool a bit, then freeze, preferably overnight, before

removing cake from pan. To unmold, dip the bottom of the pan into hot water to loosen the cake. When it will move easily, unmold it onto a cake plate. Peel off the paper and discard.

Topping: Whip the heavy cream, adding vanilla and sugar as it thickens. Mask the cake with the whipped cream and decorate the top with shaved chocolate. Refrigerate until ready to serve. Anytime up to 15 minutes before serving, puree the defrosted raspberries in a blender and press through a fine sieve to remove seeds. Spoon the raspberry puree around the cake just before serving or spoon some of the puree around individual slices.